# Real Women...
# *Real Talk*

PAULETTE WALKER JOHNSON

Produced by:

# FriesenPress

Suite 300 – 852 Fort Street
Victoria, BC, Canada V8W 1H8

www.friesenpress.com

Distributed to the trade by The Ingram Book Company

Forget Reality TV ... this is as real as it gets! Real talk from a woman who keeps it real and isn't afraid to tell you how she feels. Read and know you're not alone ... laugh, smile, say "amen" or disagree, reflect, and learn. Whatever your age, Real Women ... Real Talk is sure to touch you on some level and certainly start some "real" conversation with the women around you.

Jennifer Williamson, Program Director, WVST-FM
Executive Producer, "Real Women ... Real Talk" Radio,
The Source 91.3 WVST

Instructor, Department of Mass Communications
Virginia State University

# TABLE OF CONTENTS

# Reviews

*Real Women ... Real Talk* is an excellent tool to assist individuals confronted with issues and challenges in their personal lives. Dr. Paulette Walker Johnson's message to women is a breath of fresh air! Not only does she offer a sister girl perspective, but she provides wholesome information that is applicable to a variety of "real" life situations. As a licensed professional counselor, I'm often met with reluctance when I suggest therapy. Therefore, I recommend this book could be a first step or a stepping-stone for some who may consider seeking professional help.

*Lakesha Roney LPC,*
*Lead Counseling Coordinator*
*Virginia State University*

---

There is none more suited to deliver a work that speaks to the hopes, dreams, love, heartbreaks, and testimonies of success, triumph, and faith that real women face every day, than a "real woman". Dr. Paulette Walker Johnson is that "real woman". She is a professional, a "sistah", a teacher, an innovator, and a warrior spirit who has dedicated her life to training our young, uplifting her sisters and balancing all of the areas of her life in the meantime. I can say that I have had the pleasure of sharing that real space with her and her inspiration is amazing.

Her book, *Real Women … Real Talk* is timely, relevant, and necessary, not to academic discourse but to discussions, "real talk" about the uncensored issues that women face every day. *Real Women … Real Talk* is that authentic "sister space" that all women can relate to and feel in.

*Zoe Spencer, PhD., M.S.W.*
*Associate Professor of Sociology, Author and Poet*
*Virginia State University*

---

*Real Women … Real Talk* is a declaration that enhances the "real" essence of a reader's character and conduct. It enlightens and reveals much about the inner thoughts of women as they relate to themselves, other women, situations and certainly men. If you need hints on living life to the fullest, overcoming challenges and improving relationships, this is the book for you.

*Juanita B. Evans-Fells,*
*Author of Best Seller, Right Closet, Wrong Rack*

# *Dedication*

It is with love that I dedicate this book to my extraordinary family. You are my source of constant support, real joy, great comfort and a lot of unconditional love. My life is good because of you. For all you've given, I simply say, "Thank you."

My parents, Robert M. Walker and Elsie C. Walker

My brother and sister, Wayne M. Walker
and Gaye W. Walker

My nephews, Terryl L. Walker and Travis L. Walker

And especially my son, Patrick Wayne Johnson,
who is "the absolute apple of my eye".

# *Acknowledgements*

I have so many to thank for the completion of this book. I have never done anything by myself and this is no exception. First and foremost to God be the glory, for the great things He has done.

My beloved family in the dedication, I thank you for believing in my ability to be and to do anything.

Patrick Wayne Johnson, how lucky can one mom be? You always give me reasons to do my very best. Thank you for your unconditional support.

Sidney Williams, your presence empowers me and makes me feel special. Thanks for encouraging me to "get it done" from the very beginning.

Eurgentine "Tina" Simmons, I could never thank you enough for all you have done to help me complete this project. You typed, you critiqued, you brought food, you were patient, you understood and you cared. Most of all, you were willing to shine your brilliant light into the world and share your incredible creative skills with me. You are my first class, first cousin and you "get" me. I am forever grateful.

Much love and thanks to my fabulous Sister Friends, Russelyn Smith, Carolyn Claiborne, Darlene Peterson,

Charlotte Hazelwood, Brenda Welch, Cheryl Miller, and Glennis Crosby. I truly value and appreciate the unique relationships we share. I could not have written this book without your crazy, amazing, colorful inspiration. The girlfriend getaways, the talks at the kitchen counter, the pity parties, the late night conversations and all those refreshing road trips were the things that truly inspired me to finally put it in a book. Can you believe I finally did it?

I give special thanks to my lovely, never at a loss for words, co-hosts of Real Women ... Real Talk Radio, 91.3 WVST, Antoinette "Toni" Jackson, Kristen "Kris" Robinson, and Eurgentine "Tina" Simmons. Thank you for catching the vision of *Real Women ... Real Talk* and helping me take it to the airways and the World Wide Web with your own special brand of classy and sassy.

To my talented producer, Jennifer Williamson and her programming assistants, Melissa Thornton and Jessica Monde, I love working with you at VSU.

Cassandra Artis-Williams, my very first publicist and special assistant, I will never forget how much you helped me get organized for this book and the radio show. OMG, I'm finally an author!

To Anthony Lewis, Ernest Brown, Billy Wooten, Takein Cooper, and Milton Simmons, for all the work you did behind the scenes, I owe you guys.

I give a standing ovation to all the "real" women who have supported me. Especially those who visited my website, offered insightful comments and allowed me to share them with the rest of the world. I appreciate your candor and your support.

Thank you Alicia Smith, my publishing guide and the team at Friesen Press. You helped to make this project a beautiful reality.

And last but not at all least; I extend special appreciation to my dear, my darling, my beautiful, Woo Woo Cheerleaders of Virginia State University (1974-2010). The decades I spent coaching you were some of the best years of my life. Those experiences we shared helped prepare me to be able to write this book. You taught me so much about myself and you helped me to become a "real woman" in the process. Thank you for thirty five fabulous, fascinating, and fantastic years of sharing, caring and a little cheering too.

# *Introduction*

I had a fascinating reign as cheerleader coach at Virginia State University for thirty five years. Those years of coaching afforded me a rich store of treasures (life lessons, honored traditions, trends, useful tips, positive principles, humor and so much more). As you can imagine, I encountered a variety of real life issues as I taught, coached and counseled hundreds of diverse women for more than three decades.

Towards the end of my coaching career, I noticed that I did more "life coaching" than I did cheer coaching. As cheerleaders, the squad was dominant and commanding within our athletic conference. But, as women, we seemed to be out of sync from time to time. There were unhealthy relationships, communication issues, problems with separation ... you name it, and someone on the squad was going through it. The women I coached had changed, the world around us had changed and I had changed too. Life had become faster, meaner and my cheerleaders desperately needed a new brand of "coaching".

Retirement from coaching after thirty-five years left me with a lot of time on my hands. I didn't miss the day-to-day aspects of being a head cheerleader coach, but I honestly and totally missed talking to my girls every day after practice. Then, from somewhere, came the bright idea that I should create a website and start writing a blog so I could continue communicating with my cheerleaders and share my "life lessons". I did just that and started blogging on my website, woowootalks2you.com.

Fast forward a few months later and my radio show *Real Women ... Real Talk* with two of my former cheerleaders as co-hosts took to the airways. The rest is real woman history. The website became a hit and the radio show became a success. What started out as a venue for me to share my insight and my advice with my cheerleaders became an avenue for women all over the world to "chit, chat and yakety yak about a little bit of this and a little bit of that".

I did my best to be open, honest and candid about all the topics I posted. My blogs were filled with my personal experiences of laughter, tears and sometimes fears. I told anyone who visited the site that they could feel free to express and share their own feelings. Those who logged on to the site were free to relate, or hate, to disagree, or empathize, to laugh or to cry. I wanted the site to do what my lessons on life had done for my cheerleaders over the years. According to the Woo Woos, my post practice talks were helpful or healing, revealing, consoling or just plain fun.

And then comes *Real Women ... Real Talk*. This book is a collection of wit and wisdom that gives a voice to those who have shared with me over the years. It is designed to inspire, encourage, motivate, help, heal and amuse everyone who reads it. *Real Women ... Real Talk* provides a light hearted challenge for readers to find and claim their own sense of well being within the harsh realities, the issues and the joys of everyday living. Each page has been personally scripted with messages that are offered as supportive, empowering, healing, entertaining and most of all "real".

My goal in writing is to help women of all ages and backgrounds to rejuvenate minds, bodies and spirits in order to attain the loving peace we all crave. I honestly hope that the words in this book will speak to readers (especially women) with a clear, direct voice and invite everyone to live in their own personal truth and to always seek to "keep it real and tell 'em how you feel". Please enjoy the journey.

# *Real Women Talking ... "Peace" of the Pie*

Life is short, and it's up to you to make it sweet.
### *Sadie Delaney*

You only live once, but if you do it right, once is enough.
### *Mae West*

## Solo Joy

There is nothing quite like waking up on a weekend morning in your own bed, walking down the steps to your own kitchen, in your own house, sipping great coffee from your own favorite mug, sitting in your own comfy chair, turning on your own flat screen, watching Oprah's OWN network and beginning a brand new day all on your very, very own. Oh, oh, oh the joy of being on my own!

How do you enjoy your solo time?

*Fekeisha says: Girl … I have a five-month-old baby, so you know I just need my naps!*

*Danielle says: I walk or jog and listen to music that only I love. It calms me.*

*Crystal says: Reading is my way to relax. I don't mean the Kindle or Nook. Give me a hard cover book please!*

## Bad, Sad, Mad, Glad!

I had a party and no one showed up but me. It was a "Pity Party" and it lasted all night long. I felt bad, I looked bad, I was mad and I wanted the world to know. There is absolutely nothing wrong with feeling bad, sad or mad sometimes. Emotional pain has been given a bad name. It is not a sin to feel miserable, upset, angry, gloomy, or unhappy. It may not be so pleasant to feel bad, but it can be good for you. In some situations the most appropriate thing to feel is a negative emotion. There are a lot of reasons to feel bad and we probably should not resist. When you leave a place you love, sadness is just the emotion to feel. When you lose someone you love, feeling miserable just might be in order. When someone hurts you or does you wrong, it is more than appropriate to feel angry, sad, mad or bad.

In one way or another, we are sometimes encouraged to ignore our true feelings and push emotions aside. We are told not to feel bad even when feeling bad is an appropriate feeling. We hear, "Oh cheer up! Come on, snap out of it! Smile ... let it go." These are messages that usually come from well-meaning people who want to make things better, but they just might be making things worse.

From now on, feel free to embrace your true feelings. Give yourself permission to feel whatever it is you feel. Express those feelings and be mindful if they last too long. I actually enjoy my "Pity Parties" they keep me sane. So, the next time you feel a funk coming on, go ahead and feel what you feel. It will pass and it will probably pass quicker if you don't fight the feeling.

When is your next "Pity Party?"

*Grace says: I have a "Pity Party" almost every day, but I do know that peace of mind is priceless. It's the God in me.*

*Rosa says: I just had a "Pity Party" this weekend and the ironic thing is that I felt great on Sunday morning heading to church. I did all of my crying on Friday, the feeling sorry for myself on Saturday and Sunday morning I woke up and felt like I could conquer the world.*

*Cheryl says: I believe we dishonor ourselves when we suppress, discount or deny what we are feeling inside. My best antidote is my freedom to feel how I want, what I want, why I want, and when I want to feel it. I thank God that I can feel.*

## Don't Even Think About Feeling Guilty!

Every now and then you should indulge in something that is wicked or fascinating or thrilling or just plain crazy. I mean just let yourself go. Do something that is exclusively for you. Throw caution to the wind and don't even think about feeling guilty!

Perhaps you could stay home from work and relax in bed all day, buy something expensive, eat junk food, ride a roller coaster, dye your hair, flirt, pick your nose … whatever. Lighten up ladies! Life is too short to be lived so under control. Relax and release.

So what if you overspent a little bit, didn't you earn the money? So what if you don't want to go home straight after work, the house will still be there when you get there won't it? Who's to say what you should or should not do? Child please, what you do is your business. Most of us have followed so many rules for so many years we don't even know why we are following them anymore. We act like laboratory mice running through the maze. We are bombarded with rules from your parents, rules from your relationship, rules from your kids, rules from your job … rules, rules and more rules. We have completely forgotten that slavery was abolished. You be free! You don't have to follow the rules all the time. Please, please, please (in my James Brown voice) allow yourself a chance to really live before you really die. Beginning immediately, I will write my own script. If I want to eat chips in bed, I will, it's my bed. If I want to get another tattoo, I will, it's my body. If I want to go to sleep without removing makeup, I will, those pimples and zits will be mine.

Join me in relinquishing guilt and taking back the control buttons. No one will have the power to push my control button but me. If you offer me a rule that is not one of the Ten Commandments, I may or may not follow it. The choice is mine. The choice is yours too.

If we don't make our own rules and run our own lives now, when on earth will we? Will we ever?

What do you think about all those rules?

*Tina says: This is advice to live by. A better me equals a better family.*

*Tawanna says: My dad always told me that I danced to my own rhythm and marched to the beat of my own drum. In other words, I do what I want, when I want and how I want. Sometimes it's right and sometimes it's wrong, but I deal with whatever the outcome is because I know that I ultimately made that decision myself.*

*Darlene says: At your funeral don't you want them to be singing in their FRANK SINATRA voices, she did it HERRRRRRRRRR WAYYYYYYYYYYYYY ?*

## Kick Back and Relax

Every now and then you need to give yourself permission to just kick back and relax. Treat yourself well by

9

putting on some soothing sounds; pour yourself a cup of green tea or a glass of your favorite wine and simply and slowly and successfully unwind. You need to give yourself permission to take breaks from time to time. The challenges, the chores and the children will be there when you are done. Learn to savor the moment and sooth your soul. This is a warning and you have been told.

When was the last time you paused for your own personal cause?

> *Teresa says: As a matter of fact, I kick back and relax on a regular basis. It took me a while but I finally learned the value of unwinding from time to time.*

> *Malinda says: Child please … I find it hard to relax at anything right now.*

> *Cynthia says: Well, I take some mini vacations because I deserve them. So do you?*

## Laugh a Little!

I believe in the power of laughter. Students enrolled in my fitness classes often hear me say, "Smile, because the muscles in your face need exercise too." Countless studies have examined the influence of humor on our well-being.

*A cheerful heart is a good medicine, but a downcast spirit dries up the bones* - Proverbs 17:22. Dr. Bernie Siegel writes, "Feelings are chemical; they can kill or cure." I totally agree. The body and soul is a unit and each influences the other. Come on; loosen up, liven up, laugh a little!

Do yourselves a favor and do it today, let go of that "mean mug". Stop being so grumpy and stiff. Our emotions are what make us feel good or make us feel bad. Laughter is a shortcut to emotional health. If we can seek to find humor in challenging situations, then perhaps we can divert being unhappy, depressed, lonely, scared, embarrassed or stressed (at least some of the time).

Why not plan your next date at a comedy club? Invite your friends over to watch old episodes of *Martin* or *In Living Color*. Rent the *Kings of Comedy* DVD or a Richard Pryor tape and spend the day in your pajamas. The key to cashing in on humor is to step back from life once in a while and look at it from a different perspective. Life is serious, but it's also funny.

Want to give it a try and laugh until you cry?

> *Ella says: I have three sisters. When we get together, all we do is make each other laugh. Nobody can stay serious around us. Laughter truly is good for the soul.*

> *Misty says: Hey ... just got tickets to the Comedy Club. I paid to laugh until I cry.*

> *Lauren says: It's good to be able to laugh at yourself because others will do it for you.*

> *Tia says: OMG ... that is the secret! Okay, I need to lighten up and stop the seriousness.*

## Brand New Day

Each day when we wake up becomes an indication that life is going to continue for at least a little while longer. Waking up means that we are alive and that God still has something important for us to do. Every day affords us another potential opportunity to learn more, to grow more and to find fellowship in a more positive and productive way. Every twenty-four hours we get another chance to discover neat, sweet and new things about ourselves. From this day forward, let's take advantage of every moment we are given. Let's not waste another second that we can never retrieve.

It has been said that, "Our potential is God's gift to us, and what we do with that potential is our gift to him." Let's not settle for a limited life with unfulfilled potential. Come on, get up, get going, get busy, get blessed.

What blessing will you enjoy today?

> *Rosa says: My husband loves a home cooked meal and he has not had one in quite a while. I'm gonna cook for him today and tell him what a blessing he is to me.*

> *Ella says: I am grateful to have a job because I have just gone back to work after being unemployed for almost a year.*

> *Karen says: I am enjoying my "empty nest" now that my babies are grown and gone!*

## Happy ain't Nothin but Happy

I want you to stop apologizing for the unique things that make you happy. Our definitions of happy don't all fit the same mold. You are entitled to experience and enjoy whatever makes your heart smile. You have a right and a responsibility to find your own happy no matter where it lives. I know several women who did just that.

One of my good friends loves to come home and find that her lawn has been freshly cut. She exudes joy when she hears the sound of a lawnmower, a weed whacker or a leaf blower being utilized on her lawn. Her husband enjoys reaping the residual benefits of their well manicured landscape.

A dear sister friend gets a thrill out of coming home to an empty house once in a while. She craves solitude and delights in knowing that no one will talk or otherwise engage her for several hours. Her family understands and supports her a few times each month by eating out without her.

Another girlfriend is a queen of the yard sales. She's masterful, she's strategic and she's happy as she wakes up before dawn and spends every Saturday buying things she doesn't need.

Yet another friend devotes all of her spare time cooking and entertaining members of her very large extended family. Her happy comes at the end of a terrific meal when everybody's belly is filled. Are my girlfriends weird? No, I don't think they are, but they have found things that make them happy and that makes me happy too. So, when it comes to finding happy, always remember, "I do me and you do you!"

Are there any unique things that make you happy?

*Elsie says: My happy comes every day I wake up. Let me share this story. Years ago, one of my co-workers had started dating someone and he was totally smitten by her. I thought he was giving far more than he was receiving in the relationship and I told him. Well, he politely put me in my place by telling me, "Happy ain't nothing but happy" and that I should leave him alone. He said if he was giving too much and it made him happy, then I should be happy for him. So true!*

*Pearl says: Living life on my own terms and following my passion makes me happy.*

*Peggy says: Special times with my grandchildren bring my happy on.*

## I Surrender

Life has taught me that some things are just too hot for me to handle. There are situations that are beyond my control. There comes a time when I simply have to admit that I don't have the resources to fix the problem. I have to learn to surrender. I have to learn to relinquish control.

If I continue to struggle and try to control an uncontrollable problem, that problem eventually begins to control me. I once heard it said, "Surrender is letting go of being the master in order to avoid becoming a slave." Surrender is not a sign of weakness or a sign of giving up. To surrender means giving in and letting go of stressors for your own good. Actually, when you have done all you can do, to surrender is quite a smart move.

After trying to have a child for several years, my former neighbors surrendered and decided to adopt. Several months after adopting a baby girl, the wife conceived and gave birth to a healthy baby boy. Surrendering turned a frustrated couple into a happy family.

The world is filled with troubling situations that are beyond our control. I believe I have reached a point in my life that I no longer care about being right or being in control; I simply prefer to be happy. It is not necessary for me to win every argument or to resolve every issue. In fact, I don't even want to work that hard at all anymore. I think I have surrendered.

## What do you need to surrender?

> *Lakesha says: When I surrender things, the universe gives me what I need when I need it.*

> *Lisa says: In order to surrender, I need to give up my own will and follow the will of my creator. That always works for me.*

> *Linda says: I have a critical need to surrender my fear. I am going to work hard on doing just that.*

## Defer But Don't Dismiss

I have come to discover that in order to follow your dreams, sometimes you will have to leave certain people in your life behind or you might have to temporarily defer the dream. You are the only one to decide which one of these options is best for you. The fact that you are wired to care and nurture for others and the fact that you have multiple roles and responsibilities is an indication that your dreams might need to be deferred until a later date. Notice I said deferred not dismissed.

Why aren't you doing that thing that you always dreamed of doing? You know what I think? Perhaps it's because you want the people in your life to agree with you and buy into your dream before you get started. You want them to stop distracting you and allow you to implement what you've been dreaming of. How can they agree? It's not their dream: it's yours. The question is, do you leave them behind or do you leave the dream behind?

The status of your health, your relationships, your finances, your children, and your jobs, these are all potential "dream busters". There are legitimate reasons why you might have to defer a dream. I don't mean this in a negative way, but certain things can prevent us from being able to pursue a dream at any given time.

In my own case, I have finally reached a time in my life where I'm no longer parenting or coaching. As such, I'm now free to do things I could only dream of doing earlier. As an active parent and committed coach, I never would have taken quality time from my son or my cheerleading team to write a book. But now, it's on and popping (dream realized). I am grateful to have arrived at a point where no one determines how I spend my time but me. It would have been virtually impossible to make that statement a few years ago (dream deferred).

In the final analysis, I just want to encourage you dreamers to "hang on in there"because your time is coming. I encourage you to keep those wonderful dreams alive because you and your dreams are very important. You might have to defer a dream, but please don't dismiss a dream.

Are you postponing any of your dreams?

> *Lady D says: I am finally coming into my own ... it's slow, but I'll get there. Pinch me!*

> *Stacey says: It has taken me a long time to believe that my dreams are valid. It is a work in progress, but I dream during the day now and not only at night.*

## Who are You?

It is becoming increasingly necessary for us to determine who we are at our innermost core. Time is passing quickly and we simply must embrace the notion that, "I am who I am." We need to do a better job of living our own truths. Not the "truths" we conjure up about ourselves, but the "real deal Holyfield" kind of truths.

Break free from your self-imposed bondage and learn to love you. God knew exactly what he wanted when he created you. Look in the mirror and say, "I'm beautiful, I know I'm beautiful" and practice believing it. Ease up with the fake and phony stuff (it's truly getting out of control). Realize that long hair, fake eyelashes and stiletto heels can't change who you are on the inside. You are who you are.

Spend more time alone talking and listening to your inner spirit. Become your own best friend. Identify your personal fears and try to overcome them one at a time. You weren't born with fears so learn to let them go.

Stop giving all your love away and save some for yourself. Make a daily routine of practicing self-love for a change. Stop bargaining and begging for outside validation until you learn to validate yourself. Give and demand respect everywhere you go. Surround yourself with people and things that honor you and make you feel good. Kick toxic relationships aside and never look back. Insist on being number one or be no number at all.

Pray sincerely each day and ask God to give you the strength you'll need to start this journey of self-discovery.

Begin to take steps toward change while you still can. If you are unhappy, dissatisfied or ashamed of who you are, then do something about it and do it now. You have the power to do anything you want to as it relates to you.

## What did you uncover in order to self-discover?

*Miss T says: Self-discovery is a beautiful thing. It opens up doors of opportunity that help us accept, appreciate and ultimately love our unique selves. When we begin walking through those doors that allow us to see who we really are, we can begin to relax and cease the endless endeavors to be, act and look like anybody other than who we were created to be. We as women bring all types of beauty to the world. Here's a nugget of gold: Your beauty is yours alone and even if it doesn't mimic anyone else's beauty, it's still beautiful.*

*Digital Divah says: Most of my truth about who I am and where God wants me to go has been mired in fear and misperceptions of what other people think I should or should not do. I now have a new lease on life and am slowly becoming more and more comfortable in my own skin. At the end of the day, I get to control who I am by modeling the best of who I desire to become. Please be patient with me, God is not through with me yet! The fun of life's journey is in traveling it and taking the scenic route.*

*Candice says: I have discovered that being myself is a good thing, one of the best things I will ever experience.*

# Real Women Talking ...
# When Solo Becomes Duet

Love makes your soul crawl out from its
hiding place.
**Zora Neale Hurston**

Love is or it ain't. Thin love ain't love at all.
**Toni Morrison**

## Can You Hear me Now?

As I see it, we have been talking to each other for years. We usually get our messages across but there are times when we don't communicate effectively. If you are being misunderstood on a regular basis, please consider that how you say something is just as important as what you say.

The tone of your voice and your gestures go a long way to either support, modify or contradict your words. Your posture, the way you dress and even how you smell can negate your words before you even say them. Effective communication allows us to relate more confidently and more persuasively. Try not to let communication barriers ruin your relationships.

What can you do to improve your methods of communicating?

*Elaine says: Taking a page from your book, I'm learning to tame my tongue.*

*Desiree says: I know I had to stop bringing all of my baggage to every dialogue. Amen.*

*Brandi says: I am working too hard to improve my listening skills. Most of the time, he makes me so angry, I just want to scream. That is when all communications break down.*

## Top Ten about our Men!

For years I have wondered and I have pondered, I have strained my brain. I just do not understand. Perhaps you can shed some light on these ten questions for me. Please don't interpret this as "male bashing" because that is not my intent. Also, please note that these questions do not apply to all men - just most of them. I absolutely adore men. I just want and need a few clear, concise and truthful answers to the following questions:

**Question #1 Why don't men understand that lies don't come in colors and any lie is a big lie to us?**

**Question #2 When will men begin to respect the fact that we are emotional beings and crying is not a disease?**

**Question #3 Will men ever learn to hear us and not just listen to us?**

**Question #4 Why don't men understand the powerful affect of sending flowers regularly?**

**Question #5 When will men learn that "snooping" is one of a woman's official duties?**

**Question #6 Why don't men know that anything they do in secrecy qualifies as "cheating" to us?**

**Question #7 Will men ever seriously recognize the inherent danger that lies in gawking at other women in our presence?**

**Question #8 Why don't men help themselves by complimenting us more?**

**Question#9 When will men realize that if they treat us like queens, we'll treat them like kings?**

**Question #10 Will men ever grasp the fact that until we are happy, nobody is going to be happy?**

Those are my Top 10 questions. Do you have any of your own?

*Toni says: I am still living and learning but I have a few answers. Question #3 - men (not boys) hear us when we have that true friendship and connection. Question #5 - men do know that snooping is one of our official duties. Reality is that they snoop too.*

*Leona says: Moses left Mt. Sinai with ten answers to problems that we've been wrestling with for over four thousand years. It just might be nearly as long before the solutions you seek arise; they are closely connected to creation; good luck!*

*Tammy says: I see too many women suffer in silence and never tell their partners what is really bothering them. Many superficial marriages and relationships are maintained everyday because someone is afraid to deal with issues. Talk! If a person will leave you for trying to make it better, you don't need 'em. .run Forrest run! If you don't ever speak up, you will be forever put down!*

*Glennis says: A man will respond when a woman's actions demand respect. We women tend to do a lot of talking. After a while they tune us out. So, stop talking. Begin to focus on you, take care of you, go back to school or become more spiritual. By the time you finish with you, if he still doesn't listen, then start walking.*

*AH says: Please add to the list: #11 - When will men realize that women just want to be held sometimes without "doing it"? #12 - When will men realize that spontaneity makes us feel special and wanted? What girl doesn't love a surprise?*

## Is a Dance Really a Dance?

I once attended a delightful dance at a nice venue. The music was lively, the hors d'oeuvres were tasty and the atmosphere was perfect. The crowd was rather equally divided between couples and singles. There were plenty of men and plenty of women too. As soon as I settled in and began to get my groove on, I saw a group of men huddled in an area near the bar. At the same time I noticed several tables of beautiful women who were sitting together talking. These ladies were fierce and fabulous but the men didn't approach them to dance, not even once.

Most of the people on the dance floor were couples (except for line dances of course). Perhaps the ladies didn't come to the dance to dance. If that's the case, forgive me for getting it wrong. Or perhaps the men just wanted to get out of the house to discuss sports. Whatever the case may have been, they weren't dancing with one another. Now this particular night,

I had my own personal dance partner and I wasn't about to share (don't judge me, you don't know my story.) Had it not been for my personal dance partner, I would have been in the same situation.

As the evening progressed, I took note of a few things. Hear me out and keep an open mind, what seems to be the problem here? Why weren't the women dancing? Why didn't the men ask them to dance? Why didn't the women ask the men to dance? Should the women have danced alone? Should the men have danced alone? Was it the fault of the men or was it the fault of the women? What the heck is going on these days? Is a dance even a dance anymore?

When we go out with our girlfriends, perhaps we should go in fewer numbers. More than three is definitely a crowd. Some men say they get intimidated by large groups of women. Also, I hear some of us are a bit too uptight with the men we meet at a dance. Guys are telling me that they are sometimes reluctant to approach us because of the negative vibes we exude. Lighten up ladies, being approachable is the new sexy!

Now I know some men can "work a nerve" and make you regret ever coming out for the evening, but at least give the guys a chance. Don't give them the "mean mug" before they even approach you. Imagine how embarrassing it is for a man to get rejected when he politely asks you to dance. Men hate to look bad in front of their "boys". Remember the poor fellas have feelings too.

Finally, what sense does it make to spend hours getting yourself all dolled up and smelling good if you don't intend to mingle? Singles are expected to mingle for goodness sakes. When I go out to a dance and I am with my girlfriends, I expect to dance. I will smile, grin and dance with anything that is clean and has a pulse. And yes, when my song comes on, I will ask a brother to dance in a heartbeat. The way I see it, it's a freaking dance not a marriage proposal. Listen ladies, men are unique creatures and most of them need help. The only way we can help them, and ultimately help us, is to lighten up and let them in.

Is a dance really for dancing anymore?

*Faye says: I wonder myself sometimes. I am glad I go out with my husband and I don't have to look for a partner.*

*Sabrina says: Nobody cares about protocol anymore. Women are taking the floor and leaving men at the bar. That's why I don't go out very much anymore.*


## Just Be You!

When you meet a new person that you like and that person likes you back, there is a good chance that a relationship could evolve. If it does, I want you to please remember that a new relationship is not a conference; therefore, you have nothing to gain by sending your representative. I want you to avoid the temptation of putting on a front and pretending to be someone you are not. Try desperately not to sell yourself out and display behaviors that are not yours. Simply put, when you meet someone new ... just be you.

Too often we want so badly to impress the other person that we abandon the very things that made us attractive in the first place. That "someone special" was attracted to you, not your representative.

If you're asked whether you have traveled extensively and you know you have never crossed the state line, just say, "No I haven't but I'd like to someday."

If that special someone likes to Jet Ski and you detest salt water, are deathly afraid of sharks and can't swim - don't lie. You could be putting your life at risk and could possibly drown if you lie, tell the truth.

If that significant other is a gourmet cook and you know the only thing you can make for dinner is a reservation at a local restaurant, just say, "I can't cook." Cooking is not one of the Ten Commandments.

If that new person in your life decides to cut back on eating red meat, please don't suddenly become "Miss Vegetarian". You know darn well you don't like vegetables that much.

If they happen to speak several different languages and you still struggle with English grammar, why lie about how fluent you are? At least you know how to say, "French fries" and "Italian sausage".

If that love interest wears designer labels and has expensive taste, don't suddenly give up all your bootleg, knockoff, Body Central and Rue 21 outfits. "Child please", you know you're on a tight budget. Do you get my point? Learn to live in your personal truth from the very beginning of any relationship. Be true to you and save yourself some time, some money and perhaps some embarrassment too.

You are who you are and that should be good enough for anyone who truly wants a healthy relationship with you.

Have you ever sent your "representative" to a new relationship?

*Jennifer says: Yes I have but I can't figure out why. I used to take on all of my former boyfriend's traits. I hate the fact that I turned into someone other than the girl he met and fell for initially.*

*Sylvia says: You got me with this one … my sister used to tease me about that very thing. I guess she was right but I didn't realize it.*

*Sandra says: I never like to reveal my true self until I am sure I want to be in a relationship. Is that the same as sending a representative?*

## No Sense in Defense

Our love relationships are often given various names. Sometimes we refer to them as being on the same team, "My new sweetie and I make a fantastic team." Be very careful not to take the team concept too literally. Teams compete and someone always wins and someone always loses. Genuine teams require an offense and a defense; however, taking sides in a love relationship can have detrimental effects. Let's stop "sparing" with our partners as if we are in a boxing match. Quit devising strategies to win as if you are playing a game. There is no place for defense in a love relationship. When partners "team up" everybody wins.

How are you going to take one for your "team"?

*Jill says: This is so true. Do you know me and my boyfriend?*

*Maria says: Been there, done that, won't do that again. I got so tired of competing. It feels good to just flow and let go.*

## Halves and Halves Not

I will scream if and when I hear one more person describe a marriage as a time "when two become one" or "when two halves become one whole". Perhaps it's just me, but I have not seen any half people walking around looking for mates. A marriage should be a union of two individuals that are whole and complete in every way. It's no wonder we keep hearing about marriages that fail and divorce rates that skyrocket. If one of the individuals in a marriage goes to work, does that leave a half person home alone? I see why some partners are described as "needy". If half of me threatened to walk away, I think I would be quite "needy" too.

Getting married?

> *June says: Really never thought about like that until now. This makes a lot of sense to me.*

> *Helen says: I just got married a few months ago. We were careful to write our own vows for this very reason.*

## Breakup but Don't Breakdown

More than a few of us have been in relationships that ended before we were ready for them to end. Relationships change and sometimes they die. That's called breaking up and as the song says; breaking up is hard to do. That song should have included a line that says; while breaking up is hard, sometimes we've just got to do it. What we've got to learn is how to breakup without having a breakdown.

Getting dumped is not a pleasant thing. It feels horrible and getting over it takes time. But time and talk are mighty healers and if you try especially hard, you can come through with flying colors.

Here are points that can help you to get through your breakup without having a breakdown.

1.  Practice concentrating on all of his or her bad points (ugly feet, can't cook, snores) and never think about the good.

2.  Celebrate the fact that you still got a chance to snag a "hero" now that you're no longer coupled with a "zero".

3.  Remember you've got one less phone call to answer and one less egg to fry, one less skid mark to wash and one less time to hear a lie.

4.  Don't make up excuses to see him or her and do not stalk on social media.

5.  Imagine their new love interest is as ugly as sin.

6.  Cry as much as you need to, but never let your ex see you cry.

7.  Start going out of town often and make sure someone tells him or her.

8.  Talk, talk and talk some more to someone you trust.

9.  Exercise and concentrate on improving yourself physically. This will make you feel better and help you get ready for your next love.

10. Keep in mind that if that relationship had been "the one", it never would have ended.

Finally, strive to concentrate more on choosing healthier relationships to begin with, and then breaking up would truly be hard to do.

What will you do to avoid breaking down if you ever have a breakup?

> *Thomasine says: I have a rule; cry for an hour, get dressed up in my prettiest outfit and go shopping. This cures anything and keeps me from breaking down.*

> *Pamela says: Sometimes the breakup is the blessing!*

## Wake up Cinderella!

Like most little girls of my generation, I had a vivid imagination and I loved fairy tales. I would spend hours reading and imagining that I was the pretty main character and that everybody wanted to love and protect me. The story of Cinderella was my absolute, all time favorite. I thought it was so cool the way Cinderella eventually got the victory over those "mean girls" who hated her and treated her so badly for no apparent reason. I was amazed by the handsome prince's unrelenting spirit as he hunted and searched against all odds until he finally found his beautiful, sweet, precious Cinderella. Oooooowee ... what a love story! What a happy ending! Well guess what? That fairytale messed me up for life. What a shame. Poor little innocent me, my first thoughts on love and romance were based on a lie. Go figure, could that be the reason why I have been characterized all my life as a "hopeless romantic"? Is that why I'm such a dreamer?

Is that the reason I can conjure up romantic stories that would put the traditional fairy tales to shame? Mmmmmm ... even now I sometimes create love stories in my mind and hope someone will figure them out and activate them for me (yeah right). I know Cinderella is to blame for this. Shame on you Cinderella!

Truth be told, it is wonderful to imagine and conjure up stories about love and romance. It's all right to hope and dream about a handsome prince, but seriously, knowing what I now know about love and romance, it's time for "Cinderella" to wake up, smell the coffee and realize that this stuff is no fairy tale. Wake up Cinderella!

## Are you asleep and waiting for a "CinderFella" to rescue you?

*Maya says: What I had to come to terms with was this: The reality is not a nightmare just because it's not "the dream". Learning to look around and count what I do have, finding real love in places in my life that weren't necessarily the dream or Cinderella romance (like the love of my children, family and friends). Waiting on unrealistic fairytales to just happen and being depressed because they don't will drive you crazy! Someone once told me: When doors close and life doesn't give you what you want, Praise God in the hallway until another one opens! Master the hallway praise! Your happy ending is coming!*

*Tina says: When I was a child, I loved fairy tales and believed in Santa Claus, the Tooth Fairy, Easter Bunny, Tinker bell and more. They were fun and safe to believe in when I was a little girl. These characters gave me a safe fantasyland and helped me to grow my creativity and imagination. Fairy tales are a temporary fantasy, but God gave me talents to write my own script with his love, guidance and forgiveness. Unlike fairy tale princesses, I help and support other "damsels in distress". Wake up and follow your heart, discern your truth, walk in your calling!*

*Justine says: I'm not waiting anymore. I used to believe in all of that mess but my eyes were opened. Oh happy day!*

*Jessica says: My prince came but he was broke and I wasn't his only Cinderella.*

## Safeguard That Heart

As soon as my home security system was installed, I felt a clear sense of relief. I felt that my belongings were protected and I could relax knowing everything inside my house was safe and secure. I really wish I could have purchased a system like that to guard and protect my heart over the years.

Think about this, would you open the door to your home and allow entrance to a person who had previously stolen from your neighbor? Would you willingly allow a thief to gain entry into your humble abode? Would you disarm your security system, invite a burglar into your private space and close the door behind him? Would you? Huh? Would you? Of course not! Sounds ridiculous doesn't it?

Then please explain to me why we let known players, certified heart breakers and thieves of the heart into our personal space? Why aren't we more careful when it comes to affairs of the heart? Why are we so eager to invite "emotional burglars, emotional robbers and emotional thieves" into our lives? Why do we willingly and knowingly permit "smooth criminals" to commit heinous crimes and take emotional advantage of us?

Why are we willing to safeguard our homes quicker than we are willing to safeguard our hearts?

Perhaps we should take pointers from security companies like Brinks or ADT and begin to do a better job of safeguarding our hearts. We need to be more diligent and vigilant, be more aware and protect our perimeters. Always remember that robbers rob, thieves steal, burglars take - that's what they do. He stole from her heart and he will steal from your heart too.

Have you ever given the key to your heart to a thief? Did you get robbed?

*Vicki says: I sure did give my key away and got ripped off in the process ... that joker left me high and dry. But I got my high tech alarm system installed now and I am ready to rumble.*

*Connie says: I got robbed a time or two. We seem to lose ourselves and forget how easy it is get your heart broken. As I got older, I also got wiser.*

*Keisha says: Some people don't want to be alone so they forget to put the alarm on. I really think that once that other person does something cute and sweet, we tend to overlook the wrongs and hope that things will get better. After you've been robbed a few times, you learn and if you don't, it's your own fault.*

*Robin says: I think I got caught up in the idea of being in love and lost myself for a while. There are definitely a lot of smooth operators out there.*

## Asking the Stuff that's Tuff

When you begin any new relationship, please don't be so happy, so impressed, so smitten or so darn scared that you forget to ask the tough questions. My experiences have definitely taught me that asking pertinent and specific questions at the appropriate time can set your new relationship on the right course or doom it forever.

Whether you want to believe it or not, every person enters a relationship with some type of an "agenda". Most people deny having one, while others dispute its importance all together. Do not listen to them and do not be fooled. Trust me, everybody has an "agenda", I certainly do and you should have one too.

Having an "agenda" simply means you at least have some idea of what you want from the relationship. An "agenda" outlines your expectations of the other person. If you have no expectations, then why waste your time and energy establishing a relationship in the first place?

Too often, women are afraid to put forth an agenda for fear it will turn a man away. Oh well, if asking for the answers to my questions turn him away, then all I can say is, "Bye, bye baby, baby, bye, bye."

Here is a list of the questions that appear on my "agenda". I ask the tough questions early and I ask for specifics. I request clear, concise and detailed information. My list includes, but is certainly not limited to the following "agenda" questions:

1. Are you married?

2. Do you have children? How old are they? Do they live with you?

3. Are you a practicing Christian?

4. Do you attend church regularly and will you go to church

with me?

5.   Who did you date last and is she/he angry, demented or psychotic?

6.   Is there anything or anyone in your past that will negatively affect our relationship?

7.   How would your former partner describe you?

8.   Do you have good credit? What's your FICO score?

9.   What caused an end to your last relationship?

10.  Do you smoke? Are you drug free?

Feel free to peruse my agenda and use my questions. Asking the "stuff that's tuff" works for me and it just might work for you too.

*Do you ask any of my questions? Do you have any questions of your own?*

*Justine says: I always ask about that criminal record.*

*Kalicia says: Numbers 1 and 2 are on my list too.*

## Love and Baseball

If you are as "old school" as I am, you just might remember a song by the Intruders called *Love is like a Baseball Game.* That was once my favorite song and I used to play it over and over and over again on my record player. I listened, lip-synced and danced to that song for years without ever truly understanding the words. Well, well, well, I finally learned the meaning of the words and the Intruders got it all wrong. Love and baseball don't have a thing in common. Regardless of what the Intruders told you, let me make it perfectly clear that love is not like a baseball game and this is why:

• Baseball has nine players on a team. In love, I don't want any players on my team.

• Baseball allows three strikes before you are out. In love, if you even look like you want to strike me, you are out.

• Baseball has a head coach who makes all of the important decisions. In love, decision making should be shared.

If you ever see those Intruders, tell them they got it all wrong and they got some explaining to do.

# *Real Women Talking ...*
## When Life's a Drag

Trust yourself, think for yourself, act for yourself, be yourself. Imitation is suicide
### *Marva Collins*

You may encounter many defeats, but you must not be defeated. In fact, it may be necessary to encounter the defeats so you can know who you are, what you can rise from, how you still come out of it.
### *Maya Angelou*

## Tame that Tongue

I am not trying to act like the speech police, but sometimes we need to stop saying some of the things we say to each other. There are times when it's in our own best interest to pause and activate some type of verbal filter.

We should recognize the fact that the tongue is a mighty weapon; therefore, we should be far more careful about what we say. Simply put, we need to "Tame that Tongue".

As a child, I used to chant, "Sticks and stones might break my bones, but words can never hurt me." Yeah right, what a lie that was.

Sticks and stones do break bones, but unfortunately words break spirits. And broken spirits are much harder to heal than broken bones.

Recently, I became painfully aware of how much "words can hurt". A situation occurred and I have yet to fully recover, but it certainly prompted me to "tame my tongue". I'm sure I have hurt more than a few people with my careless choice of words over the years. For that I ask forgiveness and promise do to better as I move forward.

I promise to "Tame that Tongue" by recognizing the following:

I do not have the right to say anything I feel like saying to another human being.

Just because I think it, does not mean I have to say it.

Any words I deliver from my mouth should be aimed at encouraging or complimenting someone.

I will think a little longer before I speak and if I make a mistake, I will be quick to say, "I am sorry."

## How do you plan to tame your tongue?

*Olivia says: A sixth grade teacher (Mrs. Grace Jones) told us that the most dangerous and most powerful weapon ever created was the tongue. I will never forget what she said.*

*GodzDeevah says: My wise old granny who raised me used to say, "If you don't have something nice to say, don't say anything at all."*

*TeaJai says: Many times, I wished I would let my tongue have its say. Many times (way too often) from childhood, till now, I've held back my tongue. I did not want to hurt anyone. I didn't know how to best express myself. However, when I get to that breaking point, "The Renee" (my alter ego) in me comes out. I would love to find a way to keep my tongue tamed, manage the appropriate time and way to release the tongue and keep a lid on "Renee".*

*Cheryl says: I simply try to apply the old expression, "Think before you speak." If we must speak what is on our mind and heart, then be careful to do it with people who honestly care about our well-being.*

*Toni says: My goal has definitely been to tame my tongue because I've learned the hard way to "never say something once that you wouldn't say twice".*

## Uncomplicate Your Life!

Have you been feeling a little pressure lately ? I'm here to tell you that most of the pressure we feel in life is self-imposed. Yes, I said it, self-imposed. That means you are doing it to yourself. Why do we continually put more pressure on ourselves than is necessary? We think and worry too much. If something is wrong with your life, then please know that there is a solution. You might not like the solution, but there is a solution. Make a decision and move on it. If you make a mistake, okay, back up and try again. Pencils have erasers because we are going to make mistakes sometimes. Forgive yourself. Ease up. It really isn't that serious. Whatever is happening to you has already happened and been resolved by someone else. You are not the first to encounter an issue. Instead of running away from the problem; run towards a solution. Look that "demon" in the eye and remember who you are. Say aloud, "I am a mighty warrior and I can do all things through my creator." And please remember that this too shall pass.

What is your plan to uncomplicate your life?

*Natalie says: Dwelling on the things that you cannot change, only clogs your mind and blocks your blessings. Often times we forget that we are strong "black" women and we are in control.*

*Parish says: This is so true, but it isn't easy getting it through to some people.*

*Tasha says: I agree with you and understand this concept very well. Unfortunately, I fellowship with a number of women who have very low self-esteem. I am going to share this information with my women's group.*

## Check Yourself Before You Wreak Yourself!

Sometimes we become entirely too attached to things and stuff. Unhealthy attachments can control us just like addictions. When we are too attached to something, we begin to feel as though we can't live without it. We believe our well-being is based on maintaining that attachment. The attachment could be to a person, place or thing. In fact, we can become attached to just about anything.

I know a woman who has an unhealthy attachment to her job. Her identity and her sense of well-being depend totally on that job. It is all she talks about and it seems like it just might be all she thinks about. I fear she could become suicidal or depressed if she ever lost her almighty job.

I also know a man who is far too attached to his car. He treats his vehicle as if it's a person. He spends more money than he can afford on gadgets and accessories for his ride. As a matter of fact, he takes better care of his car than he does his wife.

Then there are those who are far too attached to a sports team. Unrealistic devotion to sports has negatively affected more than a few interpersonal relationships. Being a good fan doesn't mean you have to become a fanatic.

Now don't misunderstand me, all of us are attached to something. A healthy connection never hurt anybody. However, when attachments persist until they become addictions, we stand in danger of losing control. Be careful; don't let your attachment dictate who you are. Perhaps you had better check yourself before you wreak yourself.

What are you attached to in an unhealthy way?

> *Justine says: I have an unhealthy attachment to my clothes and I plan to work on it.*

> *Gladys says: My issue is food. We all have to eat don't we? I am working on it.*

> *Mary says: Work consumes me and I can't seem to step away from it. I need to.*

> *Dominique says: Until recently, it was the relationship with my child's father that I was too attached to. I finally let that go and never intend to go down that road again. Sharp scissors, strings cut. Whew!*

## Rewind and Reset

I am grateful for the fact that I have been given a lot of second chances in my life. I have failed or fallen short more than a few times. In fact, in some cases, I have been given third and fourth chances. The failures I experienced have been in both my personal and my professional life. I'm not alone; everyone fails at one time or another at one thing or another. Failing is an absolute fact of life that none of us can avoid. The issue is not whether you or I will fail, but what we do with that failure once we experience it.

I have learned that I must be willing to accept my failures and learn from them. Failure can be one of life's greatest teachers. Failing comes with the territory on the road to success. Some of my greatest blessings, lessons and rewards have come after I attempted something and failed. I eventually learned to assess what happened, then to rewind, reset and change my course of action. Starting over with a clean slate is a good way to keep moving forward. The ability to rewind and reset reminds me that real success rarely comes on the first attempt. Success at anything requires quality time and sincere effort.

Is it difficult for you to rewind and reset after failure?

> *Anna says: No, not for me. I do it on a regular basis dealing with challenging ("crazy") people every day.*

> *Pacing says: Yes, it's easier said than done. Got an APP for that?*

## Get Over It!

The fact is, some bad things have happened to us. Those things hurt us and should never have occurred. We didn't deserve what happened and it was not our fault.

The good news is, you survived. I survived. We survived. We didn't die. We lived through those experiences. It is now time to let go of our harmful past and get over it.

Now, not later, is the perfect time to stop reliving, revisiting and reviving those negative feelings. It's over, it's in the past. We made it. Praise God. Every time your mind wanders back to a painful or hurtful experience, stop, think and meditate on something good. The mind cannot process a negative thought and a positive thought at the same time. We have the power to control what we think. Holding on to past hurts does us more harm than it does the person who caused them. The other person has moved on, shouldn't we move on too?

You will begin to heal and feel better if you identify and list the positives in your life. You probably have far more than you think you have. Keep your list of positives handy and review it regularly. When you feel tempted to revisit that negative place, stop, check your list of positives and keep on moving. In the tradition of "strong women" we must learn to heal ourselves or sometimes we will remain sick forever. Let the healing begin.

Aren't you sick and tired of being sick and tired?

> *Carol says: Yes, and I am too tired to do anything about it but I will ask my God and my girl friends to help me.*

> *Daphne says: I am sick and tired and I want to do better, just for my kids.*

## Grab the Bull by the Horns

Most people try everything within their power to avoid pain. Sure, none of us particularly likes pain but we can't get through life without it. Case in point, your mother endured tremendous pain so you could be born. You likely fell and hurt yourself hundreds of times before you finally learned to walk or ride a bike. The list goes on and on.

I have come to recognize that pain is a necessary part of my life. Life has shown me that the quicker I acknowledge pain and move through it and stop trying to move around it, the better off I will be.

For example, if you experience a toothache you already have a painful problem. The longer you postpone going to the dentist, trying to avoid the pain, the worst the situation becomes. What could have been a routine extraction becomes an expensive root canal or even worst, an infection.

The point I'm trying to make is, you are going to experience pain in your life. Life's pain can be physical, mental or social. Seek to understand your pain, accept your pain and prepare for your pain. When the pain comes, attack it quickly and precisely. You cannot get through it, until you go through it.

My Grandpa used to say, "Grab the bull by the horns."

If any of you have ever seen a bull, grabbing one by the horns does not seem like a smart thing to do. However, that is exactly what you must do. If you are holding a bull by the horns, the bull certainly can't stick his horns in you nor can he run over you (after all, you are on top of his head, holding his horns, looking him in the eyes). While starring the bull in the face is an awfully scary position to be in, you are not going to get hurt unless you panic and let go. In other words, get up close and personal with things that scare you the most. Take your pain and problems head on, keep a watchful eye on them and ride them out until they subside. Don't run from your pain, accept it, learn from it, and keep on living.

Have you ever grabbed a bull by the horns ... how did you ride it out?

*Elsie says: It was my daddy that gave that advice. "Pa" had a lot of wisdom and he didn't mind sharing it. I never forgot that story about grabbing the bull by the horns and I shared it with* my daughter. "Pa" was making the point of how important it is to tackle a problem head on and stop putting things off. It's a strategy that works for my daughter and for me too.

Wanda says: I always try to tackle my problems one at a time and in the order of importance to me. I guess I grab the bull by the horns too.

Paulette R says: I learned that valuable lesson over thirty years ago. I was a female supervisor in a male dominated field. I grabbed bulls every single day.

## Drop Down and Get Your Eagle On!

*I once watched a beautiful eagle perched high in a tall, tall tree,*
*I spent months watching that eagle*
*because that bird fascinated me*
*It was always alone, it looked focused and fierce*
*I saw it hunt food as it dove and pierced*
*It relied on instinct and was always alert*
*That eagle rarely made mistakes and it rarely got hurt*
*If I were a bird, an eagle I'd be,*
*Do you think that reveals anything about my personality?*

I have no idea when my fascination with eagles began because during my early childhood days, the birds I saw most often were ordinary barnyard chickens. I don't remember seeing an eagle until I became an adult. My maternal grandmother lived on a farm and raised chickens and sold their eggs for extra money. Grandma fed and protected thousands of chirping, non-flying, mundane looking barnyard chickens for years. Her chickens always seemed to be happy and content living in their congested quarters with nothing to do but eat, sleep and peck around in the dirt all day long. They were totally dependent on my Grandma to meet their every need. Those poor chickens didn't ever try to escape or attempt to change their situation in any way. Without my Grandma, they wouldn't have had any food, any water, any shelter or any protection. One day, my Grandma died. What do you think happened to her chickens?

Are you behaving like a barnyard bird or are you an eagle?

> *TideH20 Lady says: Of course I'm an eagle and I share that eagle mentality. I become impatient with barnyard birds and they don't seem to like me either. Oh well, such is life, some folks are comfortable being barnyard birds, but some of us like to soar like the eagle.*

> *Jillian says: After reading that story, I'm eager to drop down and get my eagle on girl! I like the analogy.*

## TOUGH, TIGHT, SITUATION

When you are facing a tough, tight, or terrifying situation (all of us do from time to time) you have two choices: you can panic or you can pray. It took me a while to get the hang of it, but now instead of freezing up in fear, I position myself for prayer. It works. Honestly, it does.

At first it may take time for your emotions to calm themselves and catch on to this strategy. But just keep practicing and before long your emotions will recognize the fact that you have decided to pray and trust God rather than to panic. In the future, when you detect fear or panic approaching, immediately bring them to God and ask him to calm you down. After a while, you'll start forming the habit of praying rather than panicking. Please try it. I guarantee you'll like it. If it works for me, it will work for you too. Remember fear is, "whack, so keep it back" and don't let it exploit you.

Have you ever prayed something bad away?

*Maureen says: Many, many times my dear, I am glad I know God and that I recognized years ago that fervent prayer does change things.*

*Nikki says: Have I??? Lately, I simply try to maintain some degree of dignity and I certainly do pray.*

*Serena says: I pray, then panic, then pray again … doing it right now!*

## Flying Too Low

I once heard a great sermon that focused on reasons why some people appear to be deliberately living below their potential. The minister made his point by using an analogy of a bird being hit by a car. According to that sermon, a bird can only get hit by a car if it flies too low. The minister further implied that it was shameful and perhaps even sinful to squander our wonderful gifts and talents. He went on to say that every one of us was born with a predetermined amount of God given potential. I have no potential to be you and you have no potential to be me. The paths we take and the choices we make in life will inevitably determine if we will or will not reach our potential. My mission here on earth is not the same as your mission. We are expected to seek and find our own, unique purpose. Afterwards, we should begin trying to live our purpose driven lives to the fullest.

With that being said, if you are not doing all you can do to realize your full potential, you could very well be in danger. Much like the bird that "foolishly" gets hit by a car, you too could be heading for an accident.

God created birds with an innate ability to fly high and soar. So can you and me. The way I see it, there is absolutely no reason why a bird should ever get hit by a car. That is, unless of course, the bird is living below its potential. Are you living below your potential? Perhaps it's time for you to step up or step out or move up or move over or get up or get out.

# *Real Women Talking ...*
## Who's in the Pit Crew?

Surround yourself with only people who are going to lift
you higher.
### Oprah Winfrey

No person is your friend who demands your silence, or
denies your right to grow.
### Alice Walker

# My Girlfriends' Skin

My girlfriends are gorgeous. Their complexions span a variety of shades and hues. Some have overtones, undertones, saturations and lovely pigmentations. They are either light, bright and close to white, dark chocolate, sand or a brownish tan. When they "dress to impress" and go out on the town, it's clear to see some colorful divas are around. They wear sexy black dresses and stiletto pumps and they are very proud of their abundant rumps. They mix, match and makeup until each one looks her very best. These colorful sisters always win, because they "love living in the skin they're in".

Having said that, it's quite disappointing to know that some women think their complexions limit their choices when it comes to colors for makeup and clothes. Honey hush! They couldn't be more wrong. There are light skinned women who feel uncomfortable wearing dark colors and dark skinned women who are reluctant to wear pastels. What a shame and who is to blame?

I love my girlfriends because these multicolored women rock. They wear the brightest bright on the darkest skin or the lightest light just because they can. They wear pink, orange or red lips on dark, dark skin and I love the way they look because I see them from within.

What are you doing to show you love living in the skin you're in?

> *Taneisha says: I realized at a young age that God made me this way for a reason. I show gratitude for my body as often as I can. When I get pimples and bumps on my face, I take it as nature running its course. As long as I see me as a beautiful young lady, it puts that positive energy around me and I glow.*

*Adrain says: I'm beautiful, I know I'm beautiful. Don't you think?*

*Chrissy says: I love me and I just keep reminding myself of that. By the way, I'm a darkskinned chick.*

## My Laws or By-Laws

 Our lives are filled with rules, regulations, and laws. We have Robert's Rules of Order, The Ten Commandments, The Bill of Rights, rules of etiquette, driving laws and so many more. Maybe it's just me, but I believe that women need some rules and regulations and laws to help govern our interactions with one another. Our relationships could be more mutually beneficial if we had guidelines to follow. As a result, I have devised some "My Laws" that could possibly become "By-Laws". Please review these ten items and conduct yourselves accordingly.

My Laws that could become By-Laws:

1.  Do not call, email, text, tweet or otherwise contact my man without my written, notarized and or certified permission. I can relay all necessary messages to him (thank you very much).

2.  Do not position yourself to compete with me about anything. Competition requires energy and I am tired of "fighting".

3.  Respect my time and expect me to respect yours. If we are going somewhere together, please be on time.

4.  Do not try to discipline my child in my presence. I appreciate your advice but stay in your lane unless I ask for help.

5.    Never talk about me behind my back. I always find out later anyway and it makes me distrust you.

6.    Stop wanting to buy the same things I buy when we go shopping. Dressing alike is not cute.

7.    Do not get angry with me because I don't want to date your weird relative. I don't care how nice he is, no, I will not go out with him.

8.    Never, ever ask to use my cologne or makeup. I do not want to smell or look the same way you do.

9.    Stop announcing that I am wearing something you loaned me. When you let me borrow an item, that particular item belongs to me for that period of time.

10.   Stop trying to drop your drama on me when we go out together for fun. Put down your cell phone and realize that there is a time and a place for everything.

## Are your laws similar to my laws?

*Renee says: I agree with all ten and would like to add a few more. My #1 is: If I tell you something in confidence about my personal life, please don't bring it up as a topic of conversation with your other friends. Getting opinions from your other friends is not necessary. I didn't need advice, I needed a friend. #2 your friends are just that your friends. I'm not obligated to be in the company of people I don't know or trust. #3 Your marriage is your marriage. Please don't compare what my husband does to your husband. I married my man, not yours!*

*Mrs. Jones says: I agree with your laws 100%. I hope my girl-friends read them.*

*Kiara says: The ten you listed are just the beginning ... we need at least ten more.*

## This Reality is Not for Me

Most women will gladly tell you that friendships with other women are among the most important in life. I would like to turn on my television and see beautiful women interacting with one another in a positive way. I would like to see a TV housewife who is not mean spirited and vindictive. What's going on with these reality shows that feature women? Why are the characters so harsh and so angry?

I long for the return of *Girlfriends* and *Sex in the City* because they reminded me of my girlfriends. We never fight and talk about one another like those reality show women do. Now let's be clear, my girlfriends and I do have some rather spirited debates from time to time (heaven knows we do). Despite our unique differences, we always remember that we have options. If I really don't want to share space with another person, if being in someone's presence truly causes pain, there is a choice. I can simply leave or she can leave.

Those "housewives, mob wives and basketball wives" are out of control. The characters are fighting more and the shows are becoming harder to watch. Most of these reality show women have dysfunctional relationships with their men and they rarely offer anything interesting or innovative in a fashion sense anymore. I am very much aware that these shows are promoted as entertainment and it's all about the money honey, but, who are they really trying to entertain? What messages are they sending? Women are not being depicted realistically on these network "reality shows". I am not entertained and as a matter of fact, I am downright annoyed. Can anyone explain to me why I should tune in and knowingly expose myself to someone else's stress and mess (things I need to avoid)? The networks should bring back women like Joan and Myra and Carrie and Samantha. I miss them because they had become my TV girlfriends and they are far better representations of my reality.

## How important are your relationships with your girlfriends?

*Evelyn says: My girlfriends have been there for me when no one else was. . They are priceless.*

*Barbara says: I trust my girlfriends to help me grow into who I am meant to be. I need them sometimes more than family.*

*Maxine says: Relationships with my girlfriends are very important to me because I am an only child and I don't have any sisters.*

## Haters are Motivators

Do yourself a favor and stop trying to get everyone in the world to love and validate you. That is an impossible goal and it just isn't going to happen. Instead, why don't you let go and move on with love and adoration for yourself? If everyone loved you, then I suspect your life would be less interesting, less challenging and less exciting too.

I have "haters" and they have been around since I successfully made it down the birth canal. They force me to take inventory of myself in ways I would not or could not do alone. My "haters" inspire me to keep my eyes on the prize and they inspire me to keep moving forward no matter what.

Earlier in my life I attempted to hate them back until I discovered I was wasting my energy on a lost cause. I am not a hater and trying to be a hater just feels wrong. It took a while, but I finally realized that I could not change a haters mind no matter what I did or did not do. They hated on me because I was alive. "Haters" hate, that's their job, that's their chosen profession.

I will be the first to admit that having a "hater" does not feel very nice. A professional "hater" can creep up from the back and knock you down in the twinkling of an eye. Nevertheless, I could always punch back by focusing on some "sweet spot" in my life to counteract the pain. "Haters" have landed some good punches and some have even knocked me down. But I would never stay down. Never did and never will. To be honest, my "haters" are now my greatest motivators.

When I can't see or hear from one of my "haters" in reality, I create one in my mind for the sole purpose of motivation and inspiration. Let me describe my most recent "imagined hater" to you. First of all my "imagined hater" has a variety of pretty clothes in her color coded closet. I imagine that she is an excellent cook and she bakes to perfection. She is thrifty and smart and she uses coupons to save money. She is brilliant, a bestselling author and never misspells a single word. She drinks eight glasses of water a day, eats a balanced diet and drives a clean, shiny car. My "imagined hater" attends Bible study and is never late for church. She has read the entire King James Bible from cover to cover and she has done this more than once. She is an outstanding citizen and gives a great amount of her time to community service. UGGGGHHHHH! Do I hate her? Heck no, I just want to be like her.

You got haters? I sure hope so!

*Cre says: The inspiration that haters give you is something special. The usually confirm that you're doing a great job being the person that you are. Haters create the perfect balance; they help you to remain humble and give you the motivation to keep your head up and keep looking forward.*

*Kim says: In the past, my feelings would get hurt if someone didn't like me or talked bad about me. What helped me is that I realized that I can't control what other people think or do, I can only control how I react.*

*Jasmine says: Envy and jealousy are some of the sneakiest emotions that we can have. But how many of us have unconsciously hated through gossip, assumptions, bad information? Every time this topic comes up we always assume we are hated on.*

*Tawanna says: Women need to stop wanting to walk in other women's stilettos, and just simply strut their own. That would surely cut down the "hater rate".*

## The Necessary "B" Who Lives in Me

I didn't want to be the one to have to say it, but sometimes, some things just need to be said. There are times when I try my level best to sit back, chill and let things go. I am fully aware of the danger of elevating my blood pressure and I do declare that being cool has its advantages. However, there are times when the "B" in me, just needs to be free.

She (my necessary "B") wants to be free when:

- I have told you more than once to stop talking negatively about my child, my family, my city, my school, my man, my cheerleaders or President Barack Obama.

- I was compassionate enough to go against my own rule and loan you the money you needed. You promised to pay me back on time. You didn't, now you won't return my phone calls.
- You insist on talking to me when I have told you that I am done talking and have begun walking.
- You have lied and you know you've lied but now you're acting like I did something wrong.
- You came into my space and disrespected me, my property and or man.

Admit the things that make your "B" want to be free.

*Shaina says: The B in me wants to be free if you try to embarrass me, lie on me, disrespect my daughter or my family, and if you mess with my money or food!*

*Lassatt says: If you don't want my B to be free, you'd better stay in your lane honey.*

## Who needs "Frienemies" when you got Friends?

If we are going to be friends, then I need help trying to understand you. I am trying to be friendly and nice but something just isn't right. Did I do anything wrong? Have I offended you in some way? I am totally confused because it was you who approached me about becoming friends. I am trying to show myself friendly but it doesn't seem to be working.

One minute your attitude is positive and your approach is soft. You appear grounded and sensitive. You seem warm and welcoming. You are happy and you smile a lot. You look like the kind of person I could really call my "friend".

Why has your attitude changed so quickly? Why was there no warning? Why has your positive approach suddenly become negative? Who does that? What kind of person goes from being friendly and nice to being harsh and abrasive in a matter of moments? I don't know who you are from one minute to another. I don't feel comfortable around you anymore. I don't think I want to be friends with you. Oh well, have a nice life.

Got any "frienemies" you need to drop?

> *Cassandra says: I had a problem with this woman who changes her attitude as often as she changes her underwear. I eventually parted ways with her before she drove me insane.*

> *Alicia says: Women need to learn how to stop being so darn vicious. I don't think men treat each other the way we do.*

## Things Every Real Woman Needs to Know

I hope every woman in the world has the opportunity to couple with the loving and supportive partner of her choice. Partnerships are wonderful and can make life so much easier. But just in case you are unfortunate (or fortunate, depending on who you are) enough to be uncoupled, there are some things you need to know. The world is not a perfect place and real women need to be prepared. This is a partial list of everyday things you must know how to do without help:

1.  Cook at least one signature meal (oodles of noodles don't count).

2.  Change a flat tire on your car.

3.  Kill a mouse, a bug and a snake (only if you have too).

4.  Defend yourself against an attack (go for the tender spots).

5.  Budget your own money and balance your checkbook.

6.  Start a lawnmower and cut grass.

7.  Turn off the main water line coming into your home.

8.  Disconnect the circuit breaker.

9.  Use a screwdriver and a hammer (I don't mean as weapons).

10. Do your own hair.

11. Hang a picture.

12. Drive a standard shift car.

13. Reboot a computer.

14. Pray effectively.

15. Change a light bulb.

16. Put a condom on a man (yeah I said it!).

17. Operate a fire extinguisher.

18. Breakup with someone safely.

19. CPR and first aid.

20. How to swim or at least tread water.

This list is by no means complete, but it's a good start.

## Doggie Do

When your doggie starts barking and trying to get your attention; when your doggie begins to scratch at the door and won't let you relax; when your doggie seems anxious and uncomfortable; when your doggie appears agitated and restless, wouldn't you likely assume that the poor animal is full of crap and needs to be let out of the house?

Well, what if that was a two legged "doggie"?

Get that "doggie" out of your house girlfriend, he is full of crap and needs to go badly. Please don't wait any longer, he just might crap on YOU!

# *Real Women Talking ...*
# *Building a Beautiful Body*

It's not the load that breaks you down, it's the
way you carry it.
**Lena Horne**

It's time for you to move, realizing that the thing you are
seeking is also seeking you.
**Iyanla Vanzant**

## I'm Perfect

I am perfect and I have the mirrors to prove it! Every day as I walk by one of the fifty-two mirrors in my house, I see my reflection, pause and my mirrors tell me this:

*I'm not too short, I'm not too tall, I'm not too big, I'm not too small, I'm not too shy, I'm not too bold, I'm not too young, I'm not too old, I'm not too thin, I'm not too fat, I'm not too this, I'm not too that.*

I am perfect just the way God made me. And if that wasn't enough, my Mama named me Paulette, because she knew the day I was born, I was going to be all that!

Go look in your mirror and tell me what you see.

*Karen says: Who said you have to be fair with long straight hair to be beautiful as perceived by the media. To say we do not like ourselves is to say, "God, you were wrong, you made a mistake when you made me and I don't like what you did and I would do it differently". No matter what we may think about our physical attributes ... God never makes mistakes.*

*Ms. Kris says: Back in the day this beautiful woman had my sisters and I recite something very profound, "I'm beautiful, I know I'm beautiful, don't you think so?" That stuck with me because as you mature and get older, the world can make you think otherwise.*

## Plan For a Better Me

In spite of all the great things that we have done as women; I regret to report that we continue to be evaluated by our appearance more often than by our achievements. I am not going to debate whether this position is right or whether it is wrong, I am simply here to say that the statement is true and here is what I plan to do:

A.   I will get my manicures and pedicures on a regular basis. When you look down and see alligator toes, it is already too late. If you can't afford to get your manicure or pedicure, do it yourself or ask your best friend (that's what friends are for).

B.   I will refrain from giving myself "bootleg" perms. If you spend $5 on the entire retouch kit and put it in yourself, you are bootlegging.

C.   I will inspect my shoes and get them repaired when needed. If you are slightly leaning when you walk, check your shoe heels, if you are leaving small holes in floors, check your stiletto tips. Shoe repairs are not that expensive.

D.   I will not wrap my head in a greasy, sleezy scarf on bad hair days. If you sleep on the scarf at night, please don't wear it outside the bedroom.

E.   I will replace my bras before they wear out completely. Just because you bought the bra at Victoria's Secret and paid a lot of money for it, don't expect it to last a lifetime. If your bra straps are unraveling and hanging under your top like a string, you need to replace it.

F.   I will faithfully use baby oil and vaseline on my legs, knees and elbows. Those cute little bottles of fruity smelling lotions and creams are not your friends. If your legs look grayish before you finish dressing, you need to grease em down.

This Appearance Improvement plan is only a beginning. It does not guarantee acceptance and isn't for everyone. I offer this plan as a start in the right direction.

## In what ways can you improve your personal appearance?

*Katrina says: I have vowed to get my pedicures and my mani-cures at least every two weeks.*

*Ricki says: Dressing for my body type, age and sense of style has freed me from the negative perceptions that I wore in my clothing choices. Cute is okay!*

*Doris says: I can start by making myself a priority. My kids are older now and it is all about me.*

## Short Stuff

In my professional arena (athletics) being short and petite did not always work well for me. As a matter of fact, my physical stature was often a tremendous disadvantage. More often than not, the visual perception of me was one of being soft and weak. As a result, I learned early on to compensate by acting strong and acting tough. My professional success, in a world dominated mostly by men, depended on my ability to present myself as fierce and powerful.

Fast forward a decade or two and now I find that the very same powerful posture that earned me so much success in my professional life has a negative effect on my personal life.

My, my, my … what's a woman to do? It's not easy to change behaviors. I worked long and hard for my fierce and feisty persona; only to find out that I now need to reconnect with my softer side.

## Has your size ever been a problem for you?

*CaRhee says: My entire life I have been judged that I cannot do certain jobs like the "boys" do but that has been proven wrong. I may be little but I have a big personality and I can also do a job better than the "boys".*

*Patrice says: I have learned to switch it up and I know when to turn it on and off. Don't test me though; I am still a tough cookie.*

## Everybody Love Your Body

Before you activate your workout regimes, before you pop in your Zumba tape, before you swear in yet another New Year's pledge to be a dime before summertime, think about this:

There are three basic body types, ectomorph, mesomorph, and endomorph. These body types are inherited and don't ever change.

To give you some examples, the model Iman is an ectomorph, Serena Williams is a mesomorph and Oprah Winfrey is an endomorph. Each of them has a distinctly different type of body. You can work out and diet "til the cows come home" and your body type will remain the same. Remember, it's inherited. Iman's body will never, ever look like Serena's and Serena's body will never look like Iman's or Oprah's. That's just the way it is.

As a physical educator, too often I see short women who want to be tall, tall women who want to be short, thick women who want to be thin and thin women who want to be thick. You get the idea? God had no desire to make us all alike. He made us different for a reason. Embrace your body type and learn to live with what you have been given. Slim, muscular or curvy; you are very beautiful just as you are. The best thing you can do is to treat your body type as well as you can. Always try to eat right, exercise regularly and stop stressing about things you cannot change. Begin to celebrate our diversity. Celebrate the fact that we come in all shapes and sizes and it is all good.

In what ways do you show appreciation for your unique body type?

> *Patricia says: Can't do a thing about what you inherit. Get over it, move on.*

> *Shelia says: I finally got comfortable with my body type. Once I got comfortable, everybody else was comfortable too. Guess what, there's just more of me to love.*

> *Tootie says: I'm an ectomorph and proud of it! Sometimes good things come in small packages.*

## In Order to be a Dime, You've Got to Make Some Change

There is no better day than today to start activating a personal fitness plan. I challenge you to start by committing to make lifestyle changes that you might need to improve and or maintain your level of health. You can begin by focusing on balancing work and relaxation, eating the right foods and getting enough exercise.

A healthy body and a healthy mind will set the stage for a fantastic week, month, year or life. Health experts (and I just happen to be one of them) advise you to get at least 30 minutes of exercise each day. However, please know that traditional workouts like kickboxing, zumba and aerobics are not for everyone. If you are searching for an exercise routine that you can stick with, consider the sport or activity you participated in as a child. Whether it was jumping rope, riding a bike, hoola hooping or shooting marbles, your favorite childhood activities can provide an exercise regimen that you will love and possibly stick with. Just remember to modify the activity, choose something you enjoy and invite a friend to join you on a regular basis. More than likely, you will have a ball and gain better health at the same time.

In order to improve your health and look like a "dime" your fitness routine should include cardiovascular, strengthening and stretching exercises. Cardiovascular exercises are designed to condition your heart. Stretching exercises keep your muscles flexible. Strength training improves muscle tone and makes you stronger. You need all three types of exercise to improve your overall fitness and reach your full "dime" potential.

Making a decision to improve your health is a personal matter that requires change. Don't pressure yourself to do anything you are not comfortable with. Remember to set fitness goals that are realistic and achievable. Be sure to select exercises and activities that fit your personality. And then, just do the darn thing.

Are you willing to make change and become a "dime"?

> *LaVern says: I have already started my fitness plan. This time I will not quit until I reach my goal.*

> *Andrea says: Rome was not built in a day but I wish I would buy me a new body today.*

> *Olisa says: I recently saw one of my college pictures and I wanted to cry! If only I could be that size again.*

# *Real Women Talking ...*
# *Super Me*

The most common way people give up their power
is by thinking they don't
have any.
**Alice Walker**

Above all, be the heroine of your life, not the victim.
**Nora Ephron**

## Don't Stay Long When the Good is Gone

It could be a job …
It could be a relationship …
It could be an exercise program …
It could be a club …
It could be a stylist …
It could be a class …
It could be a dream …

It could be a team. Whether it's a boring book, a rocky relationship or a job that stresses you out, sometimes you just have to throw in your towel and quit. That's it, end of discussion, I quit.

Have you been staying too long when the good is gone?

*Angela says: Sometimes you just don't know when the good is gone. I now know that I was staying too long.*

*Shelly says: I stayed far too long because I was too busy trying to please others and forgot about ME.*

*Gwen says: I never wanted to seem like I was a quitter. At some point I finally realized that the good was all gone.*

## She Got a Big Ole But

While some women have chosen to undergo elaborate, expensive and risky procedures to augment and enhance, I'm working diligently to reduce mine. I'm talking about my big ole but! Yeah, I have one and what about you?

If any of these seem familiar, then you've got a big ole but too:

• My doctor told me to exercise and eat more fiber but …

• My savings account is depleted and I need to stop shopping but …

• This relationship is making me sad and I should move on but …

• I want to stop hoarding and clear out some of this junk but …

• I really need to go back to school and complete my degree but …

• I'm stressed and need to take some time for myself but …

• I can't take on any more responsibilities and I should just say "no" but …

But, But, But, But, But, But, But, But, But, But … Help … my But is getting bigger!

How do you plan to get rid of your big ole but?

*Toni says: Man oh man, I have a long list of things to do and I have some really good reasons why those things aren't done yet, BUT I am working on slimming that list down so my but won't be busting out of my pants. Don't put off for tomorrow what I know I need to do today!*

*Rusty says: I learned a longtime ago to decrease my usage of the word "but" because of the limitations it imposes. I love the word "and" because it is so inclusive. Also, it reminds me that there are options, more than one way of thinking and doing.*

*Tenika says: I know I have a big, big but. In the words of my former cheerleader coach, I can get rid of anything if you just "gimmie two weeks".*

*Yovonda says: I got a big ole but, and a big ole butt! I'm working on both of them.*

## I Got Work to Do

I have decided to be the change I want to see. There is work to be done and I am going to start with me. I must do a better job of practicing the things I preach. The world needs more understanding, more kindness, more forgiveness and a lot more encouragement. Therefore …

I've got to smile when people talk negatively about me.

I've got to ignore bad attitudes.

I've got to overlook unkind gestures.

I've got to keep my mouth shut unless I have something good to say.

I've got to be tolerant of people who don't do the same for me.

I've got to find the good in every person I meet.

I have an awful lot of work to do, whew!

## Spirit Check

For many of us, the hustle and bustle of our everyday lives drowns out our spirit that speaks to us saying "take care of you". Instead of listening to that voice of spirit ,we get sidetracked and tune into the voices of others. Refusing to listen to our inner voice can cause physical and or emotional damage. We must learn to listen to our spirits and take better care of ourselves.

Some of us are mothers and some are wives. Some of us are high profile professionals or looking for a job. Some are newly separated and some of us are primary caregivers. Some are suffering, while some are students. Some are scared and some of us are just over extended. We are all doing so much and we've got so much more to do.

The truth is; reluctance to take care of oneself can cause self-esteem issues. It promotes self-doubt and insecurity. Regardless of what goes on in life, we must find ways to take care of ourselves by any means necessary. Personal well-being should be our most important goal. If we are not well, then it's quite likely that all other aspects of our lives will suffer.

We cannot continue to allow our multiple roles and responsibilities to force us to dance out of step. We must not rock or roll to the beats of drums that are not our own. Instead we must learn to step to our natural rhythm of life. We must block negative voices and stay tuned into the sounds of joy and peace.

## Shop Til I Drop

I feel blessed to be able to work, pay my bills and have a few dollars left over at the end of each month. God is good to me and I am grateful beyond mere words. Having said that, please know that I love to shop. Did you hear me? I love to shop!

As long as I am gainfully employed, at least some of the dollars I earn are going to be spent on me. That's just a fact Jack. Good golly Miss Molly, why are you so worried about what I do with my money? I didn't ask you for any of yours did I? Please stop judging me and leave me the heck alone about my shopping. It's therapeutic, I'm serious. For me, shopping is a form of relaxation and I never seem to get enough. I have never seen a mall I didn't like. Going in an outlet store elevates my pulse. I even get a mild thrill while strolling through the aisles in Walmart. I can shop from sun rise to sun set and I don't necessarily have to buy a thing. It's not spending money that I like - it's the shopping. I shop online and I shop off line, I shop on sale and I shop retail. I'm a shopaholic and I know it.

Some people love to cook, I do not. Some people love politics, I do not. Some people love to sit home and read, I do not. I love to shop. So if you see me leaving the mall, Macy's, Marshall's, Ross, DSW, TJ Maxx or Walmart, don't get in my way because I am on a mission. I love to shop. Get it? Got it? Good!

Are you ready to go shopping?

> *Doreen says: A portion of every one of my paychecks is going to be spent on me ... because I love me some me and I love to shop too.*

> *Carolyn says: Shopping is soothing and comforting to me. I just wish I had enough money to do it every day. I buy more for other people than I buy for myself.*

## Try, Try and Try Again

Who had the audacity to say that having a healthy, wholesome and productive relationship is easy? Relationships are not easy, they are hard. But, they are well worth your very best effort. Just because you lost at love once or twice or seventy four times in the past, it's no reason to give up trying.

Shucks, life is short, try getting back in the game.

*Don't you dare whine and don't you dare fret ...*
*Keep your pretty head up, it isn't over yet!*

Consider this and maybe you'll be encouraged:

- When you had that fender bender you didn't stop driving did you?
- Did you stop eating when you got poor service at the restaurant?
- You didn't drop out of school when you failed that test did you?
- Did you quit the team when you didn't score in a particular game?
- You missed the sale but you didn't stop shopping did you?

Get the point? Love is so worth the effort.


## I'm Not Your Superwoman

Pssssst, psssst ... do you smell something burning? Just relax, stay calm, you won't be harmed. Don't call the fire department and don't sound the alarm. What you smell is smoke from the burning of my "superwoman" cape. I finally burned it and I am glad it's gone. I've been everybody's "superwoman" for far too long. This is a bitter-sweet moment for me because I had grown so comfortable wearing my 'superwoman" cape. It made me feel infallible and it made me feel strong. It made me feel that I could cure emotional illness and correct every wrong. I could ward off the fiercest enemy and never miss a beat. I could jump the highest hurdle and land on my feet.

It has taken a lot of soul searching for me to arrive at this point. That "superwoman" cape served me well for many years. Nevertheless, I finally did it. I watched it burn and I've got ashes to prove it. I destroyed my "superwoman" cape and I love how I feel.

> *No more running to the rescue or jumping through hoops*
> *No more fighting worthless battles like an army troop*
> *No more leaping tall obstacles in a single bound*
> *No more begging for love when there's none around*
> *No more saying "yes" when I need to say "no"*
> *No more staying over when I really should go*
> *No more taking on burdens that are not my own*
> *No more entertaining when I want to be alone*
> *No more high-flying escapades to save the world for this chick*
> *I am not your "Superwoman, I've given up that trick!*
> *I have fixed and saved for the very last time*

If you get in trouble, you'd better drop a dime (and call 911). Your needs? Your wants? You'd better leave me alone, I can't rescue anyone, because my cape is gone.

## What are your superwoman issues?

> *Amy says: I feel like I am going through a situation right now that I do not know where to turn. I've always been able to fix*

*things, but this issue feels completely out of my reach. I feel lost
and I've been trying to get advice, but the situation that I'm
going through can't be advised by just anyone. I hold my troubles
in, in hopes of them somehow magically fading away. I wish
I could burn my cape, but I am so young, my cape is actually
a "blanky".*

*Grace says: Cape on fire. Let go and let God ... peace of mind
... priceless.*

*Carla says: I don't have a cape to burn but I do have some
running shoes. And the older I become, the more I realize that I
don't use my running shoes a lot.*

## Big Girl Panties

Everywhere I turn someone rich or famous is coming out
with a new clothing line. *She* by Sheree, *Baby Phat* by Kimora
Lee Simmons and Beyonce's *House of Dereon* are some that I
see. I may not be rich or famous but I believe my new line of
lingerie will be.

My line is simply called *Big Girl Panties*. These user-
friendly panties are manufactured in an array of colors. They
are adjustable, comfortable and disposable too. My *Big Girl
Panties* come in several different fabrics and of course one size
fits all.

An important feature is the fact that you can whip them
out, pull them up and handle your business like a big girl
should. Once you put on your *Big Girl Panties*, life as you
know it will never be the same. Your co-workers will step
aside and give you respect. Your colleagues will marvel at your
power and be more select.

No more getting caught off guard when someone approaches you in the mall. No more stuttering in a business meeting. No more whining on an awkward date. Instead, just reach for your *Big Girl Panties*, do whatever it is you need to do and call it a day.

My Big Girl Panties are not sold in stores. Victoria's Secret couldn't embrace the concept. Oh well, their loss not mine. My new lingerie is fine and it's going to get better with time.

Have you ever gotten blindsided wearing those cute little decorated thongs? I have nothing against sexy and I have nothing against cute, but sometimes, "A girl's got to do what a girl's got to do!"

I keep a pack of my disposable *Big Girl Panties* on my desk and a pack in each purse. I carry a supply in my glove compartment in case things get worse. They make my life manageable and easier too. I got a supply of my *Big Girl Panties* waiting just for you.

Place your order for *Big Girl Panties* .... No shipping fee if you order directly from me!

# *Real Women Talking*
## ... Things and Stuff

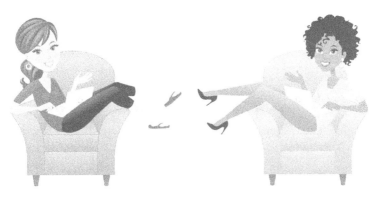

I am where I am because I believe in all possibilities.
**Whoopi Goldberg**

A crown, if it hurts us, is not worth wearing.
**Pearl Bailey**

## Single? Satisfied?

Congratulations and best wishes to every happily married and eagerly engaged person out there. I strongly believe in the institution of marriage and embrace its numerous benefits and rewards.

I am proud to say that I have been both happily married and happily single over the course of my lifetime.

"I wouldn't take nothing for my journey."

My past experiences got me to where I am today. Presently, I am a self-proclaimed, card toting expert on both being single and being married. Nevertheless, I realize that some of you are stressing over the fact that you are not married yet. Some of you are just plain tired of always being a bridesmaid and never being a bride. You have had enough of kissing frogs and waiting on your prince charming to arrive. Some of you have reached an age where you think you should be married. Mmmmm ... well, well, well, is that so? Who said you are supposed to be married? Huh?

Listen carefully, let me give you a few points to consider (remember I'm a card toting expert).

- Point #1 Every adorable couple you see holding hands, strolling in the mall or walking down the aisle in the grocery store is not happily married (can I get an amen?).
- Point #2 Being overly anxious to find a husband can distort your judgment if you are not careful.
- Point #3 Marriage is a twenty-four sev-

en, three hundred sixty five kind of commit-
ment and that ain't nothin to play with.

- Point #4 Being somewhat satisfied and single is far better than being moderately miserable and married (can I get another amen?).
- Point #5 Jesus never married, meaning he is single too. Duh.

Forget about getting married and start trying to love the
life you live and live the life you love.

If you are single, are you satisfied?

*Marsha says: Yes, yes, yes, yes ... finally!*

*Gaye says: I've been married for years but when I was single, I
was satisfied. Now, I guess that means I'm married and satisfied.*

*Belinda says: Satisfied, but not single, praise the Lord!*

## Dead and Gone

There is no gentle, cute or easy way to say this but it's time
to "pull the plug" on that terminally ill relationship you've
been holding on to.

My goodness, that relationship has been on the critical list
for years. It was extremely sick, and then it became fatally ill,
now it's over. Seriously, it is over. Your relationship is dead.

I give lots of kudos to you for being so giving and so forgiving. You were a real trooper and you hung in there for a
long time. You suffered and you endured. You gave it all you
had. In fact, you gave it 110% and it still didn't get better.

You have my sympathy, but there comes a time when the
noble thing to do is to simply acknowledge that "it is over"

and gracefully let it go. Walk away with your sanity and do not look back.

Everyone (and I do mean everyone) except you has "thrown in the towel" on your relationship. Your family gave up, your friends gave up, and your partner obviously gave up too. Look around, the only one still holding on is you.

Ask yourself ...

1. Why am I so terrified of walking away from a dead relationship?

2. Why do I stay when none of my needs, my wants or my desires are being met?

3. Why do I want to be with someone who clearly does not want to be with me?

Letting go is hard but sometimes it is just what has to be done. A relationship that is "dead" is a sad and lonely one.

Listen carefully, because you will only get this one life. Choose not to live in self-imposed pain. Instead, make a choice to bury your dead relationship and you»ll find love again.

## Isn't being miserable on a regular basis a good enough reason to move on?

*Keisha says: Yes it is ... I can't figure out why we so often settle for less when we deserve the best? Walk away from toxic relationships, turn that page and begin a brand new chapter in your life. I did it and so can you!*

*Marsha says: So true, but it is sad to say that fear of failure and loneliness seems to outweigh happiness in some cases. I finally opened my eyes and realized that life is too short to waste precious years with someone who doesn't want to be with you.*

*Teecher creature says: I agree and want to add that when you settle for anything, you block the blessings and use up all of your energy. Discard the garrbbaaage and clean up your emotional closet so you can fit the new items in there. Keep a mess, be a mess.*

*Lynn says: It should be, but some women would rather hold on to a bad relationship than be alone. Personally, I feel it is better to be alone and happy than it is to be coupled and miserable.*

## Just a Friend

If you are in a romantic relationship, asking someone or being asked by someone to just "be friends", it's often viewed as a terrible thing. "Being friends" is a role no one wants to play because it usually means the end of romance and signals that someone is ready to move on.

"What do you mean, let's just be friends, don't you know I love you? I don't want to be your friend; I want to be your lover!"

Well, I have come to discover that being your partner's friend is a good way to begin building a lasting foundation. "Friend" is no longer the feared and dreaded title it once was.

**************News Flash**************

It is friendship not fireworks that forms the basis of an enduring relationship. Consider becoming a friend before the fireworks begin. Look carefully for like before you look for love. Slow your romance roll and try being friendly, who knows, you might pick up a "friend".

Did you make a friend before you let the romance begin?

> *Digital diva says: The bottom line is; you must like yourself before you can expect anyone else to like you.*

> *Nikki says: Now you tell me! This is a bit late, but I'll eventually get it straight.*

## Better Safe than Sorry

I have done a significant amount of traveling alone. There were times when I visited big cities, stayed in large hotels and no one knew my whereabouts but me. On one particular trip I came to the realization that I was not being very smart or very safe. Someone needed to know where I was and what I was doing. If I got hurt or abducted (God forbid) where would the search begin? What city was I in? I devised a few strategies that could save my life and perhaps yours too. I know you are an adult, but these are things I have learned to do:

1.  Whenever you leave home always tell at least one person where you are going and who you are with. No one is trying to "track" you; we just need to know where to tell the police to start looking. If you are "creeping on the down low" and don't want anyone to know, perhaps you can tell a stranger.

2.  When traveling alone on business and staying in a hotel, leave a note in your suitcase whenever you leave the room. The note should answer who, where, when, what and why about your departures. For example; gone to the mall alone, left at 5pm, Red Lobster, taxi, back by 9pm and so on. This information could be very valuable if something happened to you.

3.   Don't reveal every detail of where you are on Facebook and Twitter. I know you are delighted that your sweetheart finally took you to South Beach, but too much information is dangerous. While you are having fun in the sun, someone could easily break into your house.

4.   Always keep a blanket, coat hanger, jumper cables, towel, crackers, lighter, a hammer and some flip flops in your car trunk at all times. The flip flops are for spur of the moment pedicures and the hammer is to knock the heck out of anyone who tries to jump you. The other items are fairly obvious.

5.   Do not, I repeat, do not ever slap a man. It is my understanding that they hit back and they hit hard these days. Likewise, do not shake your finger in a man's face. Some of them are stressed and have very short fuses and might suddenly strike out at you on sheer instinct. I learned this the hard way.

6.   Never, ever give a ride to someone hitch hiking on the side of the highway. Forget that Good Samaritan stuff. Politely give them the "Miss America" wave and keep it moving. In most cases, the person hitch hiking had the same opportunities to purchase a car that you had. You are not a taxi service.

7.   Don't ever start a fight, an argument or a confrontation of any type unless you already know you can win. Why would you?

8.   Never be too proud to beg. "Please mister, please don't hurt me, I will do anything (and I do mean anything) you say good Sir, please let me live, please, please." I would rather be alive with my pride compromised than to be a proud dead woman.

9. When you sense trouble coming, leave the area before something jumps off.

10. Always look both ways before you cross the street.

These pointers could save your life.

## Would you rather be safe or would you rather be sorry?

*Azeta says: I would definitely choose being safe over being sorry. My daughter and I utilize all of these and more. I get safer and smarter each day.*

*Tracey says: Just because I leave home on a trip does not mean that I don't want to return. I generally practice safety first.*

*Lynda says: I would rather be safe. I am not hiding from anyone and I am definitely not "wanted".*

*Rita says: I used to leave home and didn't want anybody to know. I know now that was a really dumb idea.*

## Gifts to "The Man" Not "a man"

Have you noticed the traffic in and around the mall during the Christmas season? The Christmas holiday should be all about Christ. It is the day that we celebrate Jesus' birthday and he should be the only true reason for the season. It breaks my heart to see people spending money and buying gifts they can't afford. This is especially heartbreaking during difficult economic times when there are so many "gifts" we could give one another that wouldn't cost a thing. If you truly want to honor and celebrate Jesus on his blessed holiday, if you truly want to give something that will always fit and always be in style, then choose to shop inside your heart, your head and your spirit. Save your money and spend your time giving one or more of these spiritual gifts:

Give the gift of patience, give the gift of kindness, give the gift of love, give the gift of respect, give the gift of tolerance, give the gift of peace, give the gift of honesty, give the gift of compassion, and give the gift of hope.

Please don't spend your money on gifts for a "man". Instead, give all your gifts to "The Man". Try to remember that "a man" could leave you and be gone by New Year's Eve, but "The Man" will never leave you nor forsake you. That's the reason He deserves all of our gifts! Jesus is the reason for the season!

Have you been shopping for the right gifts?

*Andrea says: I used to buy gifts for men that I wanted to impress. It never worked. Now I don't buy them gifts at all.*

*Yvette says:Yes, because I also make sure there are gifts for me and gifts that I pamper myself with too. Never shortchange yourself.*

*Vanessa says: I am glad we don't exchange gifts anymore … too much pressure and stress. It should be a choice, not a duty.*

## It's a Dog Gone Shame!

I am not an animal lover and I need you to know it. Don't get all hot and bothered and contact People for the Ethical Treatment of Animals (PETA) to have me arrested. I would like for you to hear my side of the story. Please try to understand my position and don't judge me. I am a good person and l love everything that God has created, but because of my overwhelming fear of animals, I love them from afar, very far.

Interestingly enough; however, there are only two specific kinds of animals that I fear the most, live ones and dead ones. It's true, I have always been afraid of animals and it is extremely likely that I always will be afraid of them. Okay, okay, I know you have an exceptional creature that wouldn't hurt a flea, well I am not a flea and it just might hurt me. You do remember the lady whose pet monkey attacked her dear friend don't you? Ah huh, that would never, ever have happened to me because if one of you had a monkey in your house, you can rest assured that this chick would never, ever visit you. Animals don't like me and I don't like them either. Having said that, I want to make this perfectly clear, please do not bring your animals to my home. They scare me and they are not welcome.

That goes for your cute little pooch with the funny name that you treat like your child. Stop fooling yourself; it is not a child. It's an animal. Just because you cuddle it next to your heart doesn't make it a baby. It's an animal. You say it won't bite, then why does it still have teeth? You can't fool me. They are called animals for a reason. God knew what he was doing when he gave us dominion over the animals of the world. He did that because they are beneath us, not equal to us. Just because it sleeps in your bed, doesn't make it a person. It's an animal.

By the way, some of you would spend more time and money on your animal than you would spend on me. Why don't you invite me to go for a walk? When was the last time you gave me a treat? When did you ever pay for me to get my hair trimmed? You paid for that animal to get a pedicure and my toes look a hot mess right now. Well, the winter months are coming and so is flu season. Have you checked to see if I will need any shots? You needed to know the truth and now you do. You treat your animals better than you treat me.

## Is that your cat, is that your dog or is that your baby?

*LaKeisha says: I am animal friendly. I think all living things have souls; therefore they deserve love and respect.*

*Eurgentine says: I have a severe dog phobia with any size dog. When I was eight, I almost lost my eye because of someone's dog that" won't hurt a flea"... yeah right! I feel the same way you do.*

*Charlotte says: I treat my animals like members of the family because they love me unconditionally. Not all family members do that. My animals live just to please me and are always happy to see me. Sorry you feel the way you do because it is a well known fact that a dog is a man's best friend.*

## You Knew and I Did Too

Have you ever had that, I was the last one to know feeling? Ever wonder, why didn't I see that coming? How was I so blind? Truth be told, you did see it coming. In reality, you weren't blind at all. In fact, you were likely the first to know. Allow me to explain. As human beings one of our greatest weaknesses is selective perception. We tend to see only what we would like to see. Using selective perception in our relationships has been the root of much heartache and great pain. Selective perception is a close relative of denial. It allows us to delay the inevitable a little while longer. No true disaster ever comes without some type of warning. Warnings often are sent to help us prepare for what's to come. Unfortunately, too often we employ our selective perception and ignore the warning signs. And then disaster strikes. It's that darn selective perception.

Why is it that sometimes we don't believe the truth when it's staring us in the face?

*Toni says: Sometimes selective perception feels good and eases the pain momentarily. God speaks and we often hear that little inner voice but pick and choose when to listen and act on it.*

*Deborah says: Just plain dumb … no other way to say it!*

*Kim says: Sometimes a good lie feels so much better than a bad truth.*

## "Triple A" Insurance Policy
## (Association, Attitude, Appearance)

Sometimes life does not work for us because we have no life insurance. Consider my "Triple A" insurance policy because without it, you are too high a risk. The premiums are low and the benefits are high. Sign up today, it just might make your life a little easier and a lot more fun. The policy includes the following: Association, Attitude, and Appearance.

| Association | Surround yourself with happy people. |
|---|---|
| | What you think about yourself shows through in the people you choose to be your friends. |
| | The actions of the people in your life can and will determine your own actions. |
| | Association brings on assimilation |
| Attitude | Maintain a positive attitude in the midst of distractions, challenges and oppositions. |
| | Patience, persistence and being positive will produce results. |
| | "Whether you think you can or think you can't, you're right." Henry Ford |
| | "Your attitude today determines your success tomorrow." Keith Harrell |

|  | Keep and cultivate an attitude of gratitude. |
|---|---|
| Appearance | Take time to take care of yourself. |
|  | You live in a society that is driven by image, do drive your image carefully. |
|  | Smiles are not expensive, give them away. |
|  | Stand up straight and always smell good. |

Are you ready to get insured?

*Joy says: My mother always told me that you are always judged by the company you keep. She also said that the outside appearance matters more than you think.*

*Jewel: It's sad but it is so true. Cute wins out over ugly, every time.*

## Lazy Ladies

You are lazy and so am I. Take a look around your house, your office or your car. Everywhere you turn there is something designed to prevent you from doing work. We have finally reached a time where we have invented and experimented ourselves into a state of laziness. We have devices to do our work for us. We push buttons to do this and we give commands to do that. We are lazy and I am here to tell you, we'd better do something about it.

The world has become so automated and digitalized, to the point where we don't get to use our muscles very much anymore. We could go an entire day without moving a muscle. No wonder obesity has reached epidemic proportions. Unless we factor exercise into our daily lives, there is a good chance that we might not get very much. Here is a short list of some labor saving devices that are helping to bring us down:

- Nu wave and microwave ovens (we don't have to prepare meals anymore).
- Self-propelled and riding lawn mowers (sling blades were good for the biceps).
- Escalators and elevators (where did the stairs go?).
- Vacuum cleaner robots (remember when the Jetsons seemed weird?).
- Automatic pool cleaners (do handsome pool boys even exist anymore?).

A high percentage of women die each year from diseases caused by inactivity. Many of these deaths could be prevented if we would simply give up some of our handy, dandy labor saving devices. We could turn this obesity thing around if we get up off our "rusty dusty" and do the work ourselves.

I hope you understand that your labor saving devices will not prolong your life.

## Better Judgment

One of the many great things that I love about God is that he allows us to make our own decisions. He gives us simple instructions and he waits for us to decide whether or not we want to adhere to them. I really, really, really like God. He distinctly instructed us to be careful about how we treat others, because it will come back to us. According to the Contemporary English Version of the Bible (Luke 6:37), don't judge others and God won't judge you. Then why on earth do we continue to point fingers, place blame and condemn others? That is not what God told us to do. Our time would be much better spent looking at our own shortcomings, instead of looking at the shortcomings of others. I hereby declare that only God will judge me; therefore, until and unless you have:

- Completed undergraduate school
- Earned a law degree
- Completed an internship
- Passed a bar examination
- Worked as an attorney
- Obtained a judgeship
- Taken the judicial oath
- Secured my written permission ... **then** do not judge me

Someone once told me that we don't need any more judges; we just need to use better judgment.

# *Real Women ...*
## Real Talk by Real Woo Woos

Think like a queen. A queen is not afraid to fail.
Failure is another stepping stone to greatness.
**Oprah Winfrey**

You are on the eve of a complete victory. You can't go
wrong. The world is behind you.
**Josephine Baker**

I began coaching the cheerleaders at Virginia State University when I was only twenty-three years old. At that time, the young women I coached were only a year or two younger than I was. During the first decade of my coaching career (1970s), my cheerleaders referred to me as Paulette or PJ (they seemed like my sisters). That label worked well for all of us and remained until I went back to school and obtained my doctorate degree. It was during the second decade of my career (1980s) that my cheerleaders began referring to me as "Doc" (they were proud of my accomplishment). It wasn't until much later, when the age difference between the cheerleaders and I widened, that they started addressing me as Dr. Johnson (they saw me as a mother figure). Whether they addressed me as Paulette, PJ, Doc, Dr. Johnson or simply coach, the level of respect they demonstrated towards me never, ever waned. I believe my cheerleader-coaching career focused as much or more on life and living than it did on athletics. During my final years as a collegiate coach, 2007-2010, I honestly felt more like a life coach than I did a cheerleader coach. The young women who cheered during the last few years used to stay back after practice for hours to share their personal problems, issues and concerns and get my advice. God seemed to always give me just the right things to say in order to help them navigate through life. Just thinking about it makes me miss my Woo Woos and those special times so much.

Here are personal testimonials from some of the women I coached at Virginia State University from 1974 to 2010. They were asked to respond to the question: What was the most useful "real woman" advice you received as a result of being a cheerleader (Woo Woo) at Virginia State University?

## And the Woo Woos said:

There is one particular real life lesson I got from Paulette that I will never forget. Our squad had just finished cheering at a basketball game and was preparing to leave the gym. We were the visitors at a school that was notorious for violence against their opponents. As we were getting ready to exit, a huge mob gathered outside the locker room. We were scared and wondering what would happen. Paulette, our fairly new coach, was extremely adamant about being ladylike and representing the college and ourselves in a respectable manner. She didn't tolerate fighting or arguing in any form or fashion from any of us. However, on this occasion, Paulette turned to us and declared, "When I open this door, we are going to walk out and you'd better not start anything, but if they start something, you had better finish it." Paulette opened that door with a vengeance, we walked boldly through the angry mob and they did nothing but stare at us. We were shocked and quite surprised that we actually made it to the exit unharmed. The real lesson I got from that incident (that happened more than three decades ago) was to make every effort to boldly and bravely walk toward my own fears. That incident taught me to respect myself, to be assertive and to insist on getting respect from others. I have carried that advice with me throughout my life and it has served me well in both my personal and professional life.

*Paulette Robinson*
*Virginia State College Woo Woo 1974-1976*

I can vividly recall a statement that Doc made during one of the CIAA tournaments we attended. Most of the cheering squads who attend the events of the tournament would stop (or be stopped) at certain checkpoints to clarify who they were, but not the Woo Woos. She would tell us not to stop and risk being turned away. Her strategy was for us to smile and keep it moving. Doc basically dared us to pause and look uncertain about where we were going. Her advice at that time was in reference to getting where we wanted to go in a sporting arena, but the "real woman" in me internalized that statement to mean so much more. The confidence behind a genuine smile is priceless and the ability to keep moving forward during challenging situations is what we all need to learn to do. A smile can warm a room; a smile can be inviting; a smile can represent confidence; and a smile can ease the pain of others. Doc's smile did those things for us. Since she pulled me aside decades ago and told me to smile, I have been smiling and keeping it moving ever since.

*Yovonda Ingram Kolo*
*Virginia State University Woo Woo 1991-1994*

The best advice I received from my coach was an example of how to live my life authentically. I watched my coach like a hawk and when anything happened that she believed in, she stood by and fought for it. She was very determined and sure that she would get what she went after in life. I am very much the same now. She also taught me compassion. She was a serious competitor, but her heart was also in favor of the underdog. She hated to see others being mistreated or made to feel like they were "less than others". Principles were also very important to her. In order to be in her company, you'd better have a set of your own strong principles, or you would not be in her company very long. Even though I learned a lot from my coach, I think the lesson of living life authentically was the greatest lesson she taught me.

*Glennis Singleton Crosby*
*Virginia State University Woo Woo 1980-1983*

---

The most useful real woman advice from PJ that has always been in the forefront of my mind was "be prepared to face the consequences of your actions". After quitting the squad voluntarily and missing the entire summer of practicing with the group, I decided that I wanted to ask PJ if I could rejoin the squad. While gone, I missed being a Woo Woo with a passion. I had been a devoted cheerleader, so I felt confident that PJ would allow me to come back. I was very wrong and she showed me how painful consequences can be. She told me I could not return. I was totally CRUSHED! After reminding me that it was I who made the decision to leave, she explained how the other girls had stayed. She explained that they had practiced and worked hard all summer and it just wouldn't be fair for her to let me just walk back on. As hurt as I was, I knew she was right and she knew these were harsh consequences that I was not prepared for. Thank God she gave me that life lesson as well as a second chance. For some reason, she decided to put my fate in the hands of my forgiving Woo Woo sisters who lovingly voted me back. I will never forget that we don't always get to come back from the decisions and choices we make.

*Levett Chisolm-Quick*
*Virginia State University Woo Woo 1976-1979*

The most important piece of real woman advice I got from my coach Doc, was to look at the worth of a man from the inside, not the outside. She inspired me to stop looking at things that were small issues and give a decent man a chance. "Don't run away" is what she actually told me. To this day I thank her for that advice. I later married the man of my dreams and every-thing has been a blessing because I listened to what Doc told me and I acted upon it.

*Shandra Claiborne-Payton*
*Virginia State University Woo Woo 1999-2002*

The most important real woman advice I got from Doc was to have self-confidence. When you go out, you should look your very best. While cheering, she taught us to remain focused and to always present ourselves as Woo Woos (even if a bug was to fly in our eyes). She taught us to speak up, always be in the front of the line, not in back. She gave us the mantra, "I'm beautiful, I know I'm beautiful, don't you think? All of these lessons and many more have helped me tremendously in becoming the self-confident woman that I am today. I will be forever grateful!

*Maisha Greenwood Gillins*
*Virginia State University Woo Woo 1991-1995*

I received a lot of real woman advice during my time as a cheerleader. The most important advice Doc gave me was to always carry myself with poise. She stressed to never walk on the campus grass, to be articulate (teeth and tongue) and no scarves while traveling! Her advice was great then and it still is today.

*Keisha Allen-Hailstock*
*Virginia State University Woo Woo 1997-2000*

The most important piece of useful "real woman" advice I got from coach was, "Surrender the fight! Let go and let God!" PJ gave me this advice after observing how I was continuously finding myself in some kind of battle with someone over something. Not physically, but emotionally. She told me that love doesn't hurt. Surrender the fight. Let go and let God! I never forgot it.

*Cheryl L. Miller*
*Virginia State University Woo Woo 1979-1982*

---

Real woman advice that I got from the best coach on the planet (Doc)

*Re: Men*

- If he can only be seen with you off campus and not on campus, he's most likely not the guy for you.
- If he dogged his last girlfriend, he will most likely treat you the same way.
- Make him sweat you. Don't always make yourself available when he calls. Let the call go to voicemail sometimes.
- Every good thing comes to an end, get over it in 30 days.
- I'm beau(TIF)ul, I know I'm beau(Tif)ul, DON'T YOU THINK?

*Re: Life*

- Keep God first in everything you do.
- Always look your best even if you're at your lowest point.
- Never let them see you sweat. Life is like a fish bowl … everyone is watching.
- Once you are at the top, there is nowhere to go but down. Do your best to stay at the top.
- JOY = Jesus, Others and then Yourself.
- Being a Woo Woo is one of the best experiences

of my life. Having Dr. Johnson as my coach, well let's say she was chosen by God. That was a position that God wanted her to fulfill and she did it with style, grace and much love. I am blessed to have cheered under her "real woman" leadership.

*Tiffani J. Hewlin*
*Virginia State University Woo Woo 1997-2000*

---

Although Dr. Johnson has given us plenty of advice regarding life issues, the one piece of advice that stuck with me was to not be afraid to speak out for what you believe in. She told us to articulate our thoughts and opinions in an intelligent manner. As a young Woo Woo, I was extremely shy and introverted. I feel that the time I spent on the cheering squad being a Woo Woo helped me to come out of my shell and become the woman I am today. I am grateful.

*Danita Thomas Hayes*
*Virginia State University Woo Woo 1994-1996*

---

The most important piece of real woman advice I got from my Coach was to never be afraid of change. You can't know something until you try it out. Doc was very strict about our appearance. She insisted that I cut my hair and I didn't want to. She told me that the haircut would improve my overall look and that it would also make my hair healthy. I still didn't want to cut my hair. It took a few days, but finally I took her advice and wow! I got so many compliments and my self-confidence soared. I have never received as many compliments for a hair cut as I did back then. Thanks Doc, for teaching me how to step out of my comfort zone and try new things.

*Tonya Flowers Rowles*
*Virginia State University Woo Woo 1998-2001*

---

I was particularly impressed with Paulette's passion for education and how she mentored us. She was not only my coach but also my Health and Physical Education teacher. While I was impressed with what she said, I was most affected by the way she lived her life. As a current educator, I realize that I have taken on many of her behaviors. She was passionate, I am passionate. She was committed, I am committed. She mentored us, I mentor students. The most important lesson I learned while being a cheerleader was, "It's not what you say, it's what you do and how you live your life in front of people."

*Cynthia Poke*
*Virginia State University Woo Woo 1974-1978*

---

The most important piece of real woman advice I received from my coach Doc is that being an independent woman working in a male dominated world does not mean you have to sacrifice being a classy lady. Doc always taught us the importance of having class and carrying yourself like a lady. She stressed the fact that "you never know who is watching". I thank her for those real woman, real life lessons.

*Kesia Gwaltney*
*Virginia State University Woo Woo 1997-1998*

Doc always encouraged me to set my goals high and to follow my heart. Her real woman advice was to reach for the stars because nothing is impossible. She told me that I was a beautiful person inside and outside. Doc always told me to keep God first in my life. It was truly an honor and privilege to have such a dynamic cheerleading coach and leader.

*Sureta C. Morgan-Butler*
*Virginia State University Woo Woo, 1997-1999*

---

It is very hard to describe the nurturing hugs and the looks of pride I remember getting from Doc. Nevertheless, the most important piece of real woman advice she gave me was to trust myself and my own decisions. She told me that only I knew what was best for me. That advice helped me make some difficult decisions in life.

*Ahnjayla Whitaker Hunter*
*Virginia State University Woo Woo 1994-1996*

---

It is difficult to find one great piece of advice I got from my coach Doc, but I remember these two statements more than any others. She said, "Always put God first in your life ... and ... a man will do only what you allow him to do to you."

*Keisha Shelton*
*Virginia State University Woo Woo 1997-2000*

---

The most important "real woman" advice I got from my Coach Doc was her telling me, "To keep it real." That saying has allowed me to continue to succeed because I spoke up. She also said, "Be exactly who you are." This is by far the best advice I remember. Doc always said, "Everyone is beautiful." I took this to mean that I should walk in my own light. No matter how quirky or odd we might have thought we were, it did not matter to Doc. I loved what she said and now I am able to embrace all types of people, because I can learn something from them. Prayer was the last great lesson on my list. "Just pray ... whether you are thanking God or faced with a decision, talk to him," is what she said.

*Krystle Hinton*
*Virginia State University Woo Woo 2005-2007*

The most important piece of useful "real woman" advice I got from my Coach Dr. Johnson was to always walk with confidence in and out of a room. A woman's true presence is known in her poise. I learned all of this by watching her.

*Tiffany Berry*
*Virginia State University Woo Woo, 2008-2010*

An important piece of real woman advice Doc has given me was to take pride in my appearance at all times. Although some might think this sounds vain, it actually can and did make a huge difference in how the world perceives me. You never know who you will come across in your day to day journey. Doc said, "If you stay ready, you'll never have to get ready."

*Shanna Finklin Pernett*
*Virginia State University Woo Woo 2004-2007*

The most important piece of real woman advice I got from my coach Doc was, "PRESENTATION IS EVERYTHING!" People are judged based on the way they look and unfortunately, that's the hard core truth. Doc would tell us, "Throw away those ten raggedy bras and panties and go buy yourself two good quality bras and five–seven panties that will last." I never forgot that advice.

*LaKresia Moss-Whittington*
*Virginia State University Woo Woo 1991-1993*

---

The most important piece of real woman advice I got from Dr. Johnson was to never compare myself to anyone else. Dr. Johnson told me to always aim for greatness but to be humble at the same time. She said if you know you are great, others will know it too. Dr. Johnson made me really think when she said, "Beyonce doesn't walk around telling everyone how great she is … she doesn't need to; others can already see her actions." I am using the advice and I appreciate it.

*Brittany Branch*
*Virginia State University Woo Woo 2011-present*

---

The most important piece of useful "real woman" advice I got from my coach Dr. Johnson was to never let the enemy see you down, and to always keep your "pretty". Let God handle all of your issues and worries.

*Kindra M. Boney*
*Virginia State University Woo Woo 2007-2010*

The most important piece of useful "real woman" advice I got from my coach Dr. Johnson was to be careful about your appearance. She once said, "Men are going to look at your hair and they are going to look at your butt." As a result, to this very day, I always make sure both of those areas look good before I step out.

*Kheli Morgan*
*Virginia State University Woo Woo 2002-2004*

---

The most important piece of useful "real woman" advice I got from my coach Dr. Johnson was to put God first in my life. I was a doubtful Christian when I was 18-19 years old. Whenever we cheered we would say our Woo Woo prayer and this restored my faith in God and my potential as a woman. She was and always will be a true follower of Christ.

*Diane M. Tyree Anglin*
*Virginia State University Woo Woo 1986-1988*

---

The most important piece of useful "real woman" advice I got from Dr. Johnson was to always look my best when leaving the house. I volunteered with her as a Woo Woo manager and learned so much about taking charge and handling my business. She reminded me to love myself because if you do not love yourself, no one else will. Finally, she would always tell me to put my best foot forward and never give up.

*Angela Andrews-Cannady*
*Virginia State University Woo Woo Manager 1994-1997*

The most important piece of useful "real woman" advice I got from my coach Dr. Johnson came during a time when I questioned my beauty and self worth. On the outside, everyone saw this confident young lady, but on the inside I felt just the opposite. Needless to say, Dr, Johnson always knew when something was out of order with one of her girls. I can vividly remember her making me stand in front of this huge mirror and say, "I am beautiful, I know I'm beautiful, don't you think?" I know I must have recited those lines more than 20 times. I remember crying while saying this, but the lesson from her was to love the person that I saw in the mirror. She told me that I was beautiful and from then on, I saw it and I believed it.

*Olisa Jordan Ashford*
*Virginia State University Woo Woo 1989-1992*

---

The most important useful "real woman" advice I got from my coach Dr. Johnson was confidence. Dr. Johnson was always my confidant and my motivator. She knew how to define and share confidence on a high level. Secondly, she shared with me how to grow as a woman, a person and as a scholar. It was always important to strive for success by having confidence about every opportunity that was presented to me. I want to thank Dr. Johnson for having confidence in me as a mother, a coach and a dear friend.

*Sharonda Davis Smith*
*Virginia State University Woo 1994-1996*

The most important piece of useful "real woman" advice I got from my coach Dr. Johnson was to always look presentable. Although this may not seem important to some it was extremely important to me. It taught me to always look the part. She convinced us to love ourselves and to believe that when we show love, we will receive love back. Today, as a wife and as a mother, I won't even check the mailbox without a little mascara and lip gloss.

*Kimberly Ross Campbell*
*Virginia State University Woo Woo 1998-2001*

---

The most important piece of useful "real woman" advice I got from my coach Dr. Johnson was to always carry myself as a strong, beautiful, God fearing woman. She also advised us that our true beauty came from within and that we should treat everyone with respect and love.

*Aja D. Hubert-Hogg*
*Virginia State University Woo Woo 1999-2002*

---

The most important piece of useful "real woman" advice I got from my coach Dr. Johnson was to always carry yourself as if others were watching and following you. She always stressed to us that as student leaders, the decisions we make will have an impact on so many others. She shared so many valuable lessons and I've learned so much from Dr. Johnson that it is tough to narrow them down.

*Shakira Hodges Lewis*
*Virginia State University Woo Woo 2000-2002*

The most important piece of useful "real woman" advice I got from my coach Dr. Johnson was to include God in every aspect of my life. Not that I had never been taught this before, but most people would question, how spirituality could be intertwined with cheerleading. Well that is why Woo is Woo. Many people will never understand how much spirituality Dr. Johnson infused into us. Being a member of Woo Woo is what held me together during my undergraduate years and the "real woman" advice I got molded me into the woman that I am today.

*Tierra Williams*
*Virginia State University Woo Woo 2008-2011*

---

The most important piece of useful "real woman" advice I got from my coach Dr. Johnson was, "Being a part of the Virginia State University Woo Woo's you are now in a fish bowl and the world is watching." Being a young woman of color in this world today you've got to have tough skin. My coach told me to learn to check my issues at the door before going into any class, practice, game or into a workplace. I remember her telling me to never let anyone take me out of my character and never let them see me being anything other than a lady.

*Chardon Jones*
*Virginia State University Woo Woo 2003-2005*

---

The most important piece of useful "real woman" advice I got from my coach Dr. Johnson was to understand that no one is going to be as happy for my successes as I will be. She also encouraged me to look at myself and say, "I'm beautiful, I know I'm beautiful, don't you think?" This was and still is the one phrase that gave me the confidence I needed to hold my head up high during challenging situations. It helped me to build my self-esteem and it enhanced my self-confidence.

*Adrian L. Ward*
*Virginia State University Woo Woo 1994-1998*

---

The most important piece of useful "real woman" advice I got from my coach Dr. Johnson was, "To be early is to be on time. To be on time is to be late. To be late is to be fried!" That message, given to me in 2006 at the start of my Woo journey, was the reason I was never late to any function with the exception of one practice. That one day I was late, haunts me still, but her emphasis on timeliness is with me in everything I do. I am forever grateful and I am forever on time!

*Parish Haynes-Talley*
*Virginia State University Woo Woo 2006-2008*

---

The most important piece of useful "real woman" advice I got from my coach Doc, is that "I am beautiful". During my years of cheerleading, she would instruct us to stand in the mirror and repeat, "I am beautiful, I know I am beautiful, don't you think?" Back in my college years, I found that exercise was fun, empowering and a confidence booster. Now, as a 40 plus years young matured woman, those words speak volumes in my life and have given me a tool to pass on to other women with self esteem and identity issues. As "real women" we must know who we are and know for ourselves that we are beautiful (fearfully and wondrously made by God) inside and out. We must refuse to let the world or any other person (man or woman) define our beauty. I thank my coach Doc for planting that seed of confidence in my mind. It keeps on blessing others and me!

*Tasha Thompson-Stafford*
*Virginia State University Woo Woo 1990-1993*

---

I value all the advice I got. She taught me how to always look my best including arching my eyebrows. I also remember that when it came time to get sized for our uniforms, there were only a few uniforms in the larger sizes. I once heard her say that she doesn't order very many of the larger sizes because, "No one really wants to see a big behind in a little short skirt." I never forgot that.

*Theresa Brown-Gardine*
*Virginia State University Woo Woo 1988-1991*

---

The advice I remember best was, how to respect myself as a woman. With that, came a lot, because I now respect myself. I won't settle and I never step out of the house, unless I look presentable. I humble myself because you get more bees with honey than you do with salt. She taught me to not depend on anyone. If I want something done, I do it myself. I learned how to be friendly and nice ("F & N") in order to work my way into any position I want in life. I learned to spread love. Doc taught me the vital things a woman should know. Everything I do in life now goes back to one or more of the lessons Dr. Johnson has always stressed to me.

*India Contee*
*Virginia State University Woo Woo 2008-2011*

What I have learned from Dr. Johnson is related to a statement she made to me directly. It has stayed on my mind and in my heart for years. Coach Johnson said, "Only amateurs come to the game unprepared!" This advice has come in handy during numerous business and personal situations. Whenever I go to meetings or have a presentation to deliver at work, I ensure the small details are taken care of beforehand. I even use it for dinner parties, birthday parties and informal get togethers, which require strict attention to details. It's the details that make the difference between amateurs and professionals.

*La Verne Burrus-Johnson*
*Virginia State University Woo Woo 1994-1997*

---

The most important lesson that was given to me from my cheer-leading coach was a hard and true awakening. It was however, something that I couldn't receive fully until I grew up and was out on my own. The words that were said had to be harsh, because I remember that I pretty much allowed the adrenaline to flow quick and sharp. Whatever came to my mind, I said. As a result, the decision that Dr. Johnson made was truly out of love. Love for her craft, because she said that she saw in me the ability to be a good cheerleader and she wanted me on the squad. She had a love for teaching and imparted mature, real observations. She "nipped something in the bud" before it got out of hand. I had to listen and accept or not be a cheerleader. Paulette told me she had to decide about me being on the squad because my attitude was "stinky" and I needed to "stop being a b★★★h". Those words stung me at the time and I cried so hard. She didn't really have to tell me that and instead could have cut me from cheering. Today, those words still resonate into adulthood, but their meaning is more profound. Paulette taught me how to carry myself and appreciate myself as well as others.

When I hear those words again, during times when I express feeling, interests, desires, I interpret them to mean:

- Diplomacy allows people to hear and receive what you are expressing.
- In order for the message to be heard, get rid of the attitude.
- When you express how you feel about a situation or person, you need your words to be heard, and not perceived as an attack. This strategy puts both parties in discussion mode, with everyone ready to both listen and consider.

*Serena Marks (Maisha Evans)*
*Virginia State University Woo Woo 1975-1977*

---

The most important piece of useful real woman advice I've received from Doc was the realization that "When you become a Woo Woo, you will change". Doc taught me that change is to be embraced to better myself as a young woman. She taught me to never settle for average, but always work hard for the best. Woo Woo's aren't average, they are the best!

*Deidre Trigg*
*Virginia State University Woo Woo 1997-1998*

---

The most important piece of useful real woman advice Coach Johnson gave me was, "To always be a lady ... no matter the situation, no matter the issue, no matter the cause, always be a lady."

*Nakeia Clark*
*Virginia State University Woo Woo 2002-2003*

The most important real woman advice I've received from my coach was that, "You are beautiful inside and out. You have a beautiful heart, mind, and soul. Don't you dare let anyone allow you to feel any different, or take that feeling away from you. You deserve the unconditional love you give, and get back from others, so don't waste it on those unworthy of it."

*Andrika Facey*
*Virginia State University Woo Woo 2005-2007*

---

The best advice I received from my Woo Woo Coach was that I am beautiful ... and if I work on myself inside and out, others will think so as well. She told me to be fierce and fearless or sit-down!

*Jerri Crockett*
*Virginia State University Woo Woo 1988-1991*

---

The advice I got from my coach is how to be more than just a "woman" but a woman of Christ, a woman of independence, a forgiving woman, and a woman full of ambition, honesty and self worth. Most importantly, Dr. Johnson taught me how to listen, not just with my ears, but entirely with my heart and with my whole being. That is the best real woman advice I received and I hold onto it dearly.

*Aprint Powell*
*Virginia State University Woo Woo 2007-2011*

I have taken Doc's attitude of hard work and never quitting into my life. I use it in the way I have raised my children. I have taught them to work hard. I tell them that they need to give 100% at all times. I tell them to never give up and when you feel you can't go on, you have to push through and pray. This is the most valuable lesson that I learned from my beautiful coach. She is a huge part of my life and the success I have with my children. I love her always and forever!

*Tracey Jackson-Ward*
*Virginia State University Woo Woo 1987-1989*

---

The piece of real woman information I got from my coach was an understanding of how important it is for me to be more assertive and to go after what I want. I have taken that advice and used it so many times.

*Casey Menzies*
*Virginia State University Woo Woo 2007-2011*

---

I remember receiving a great deal of useful real woman advice from "Doc". One great piece was that "it is important to not only love and uplift yourself, but to love and uplift your sisters". When I joined the squad, I was an only child. Becoming a Woo Woo was a bit of a culture shock for me. I went from being alone to having 22 "sisters" around me all the time. Doc quickly taught us that when you love like we did, it will multiply, and when it multiplies (like it did amongst my Woo Woo sisters) you are bound to get it back. She encouraged us to love and for me, that Woo love I found will never be broken.

*Carla Howard*
*Virginia State University Woo Woo 1997-2000*

One of the most important pieces of useful real woman advice I got from my coach was how important it is to carry myself as a lady. This is especially true with regards to dealing with men. I can remember during a "lemon squeeze" two of my Woo Woo sisters were at odds over the same guy. Dr. Johnson spoke up and said, "Nothing is worse than two friends being at odds over the same guy and that guy is running game on both of you." That statement spoke volumes to me because it made me instantly realize how some men view women. It was that moment that it became clear how a man could view a woman who is fully aware that he isn't being faithful to her, and she continues to deal with him. A man would likely consider that woman as weak and convenient. Dr. Johnson advised us to never allow a man to break up a friendship, especially when that man has no desire to commit to either one of you.

I also wanted to add her advice on beauty. She advised us that our hairlines should be exposed more because it brings out the natural beauty in the face. As a result, she required us to wear our hair off the foreheads for games. She made me feel beautiful and that's the way I feel today as a wife and a mother.

*April Poindexter*
*Virginia State University Woo Woo 1999-2000*

The most important piece of useful real woman advice I received from my coach was to always be on the right side of RIGHT! She also taught me to live in such a way that if God had to make a movie of my life, I wouldn't be embarrassed for him to see it. Those words will forever be engraved in my heart and in my everyday life!

*Tiara Dabney*
*Virginia State University Woo Woo 2007-2011*

The most important piece of real woman advice I got from Dr. Johnson was, "What others think of you is none of your business." It was the most liberating advice I ever received. Prior to her telling me that, I made choices based on worries of what others would think of me. Later, I realized I should only be concerned about God's judgment.

*Kyesha Savage*
*Virginia State University Woo Woo 2008-2010*

---

The most important pieces of useful real woman advice I got from my coach were that I am a beautiful woman and that everybody makes mistakes. She said if I needed anything, she would be there for me. And lastly, don't let your situation get the best of you ... make the best of your situation.

*Crystal Scott*
*Virginia State University Woo Woo 2000-2001*

---

The most important piece of useful real woman advice I got from my Dr. Johnson was, "To not let anyone define who I am and to love myself." I was going through a hard time in a relationship and Doc helped me realize that I should not depend on other people as a source for my own happiness.

*Elizabeth "Lizz" Robbins*
*Virginia State University Woo Woo 1993-1997*

Dr. Johnson emphasized the importance of taking pride in our appearance. I carry with me the principle that my outside appearance is often viewed as a reflection of my character, esteem, and confidence. This very lesson has helped me propel academically, and professionally. In summary, I will always remember her saying, "Look the part."

*Precious Harrison Williams*
*Virginia State University Woo Woo 2005-2007*

---

The most important piece of real woman advice I got from my coach was that no matter where you go, always make sure your hair and make-up are done. Whether we believe it or not, people judge us first on appearance. Never give them an opportunity to wrongfully judge. Also, don't ever put parts in your flowing hair because you will look like a wretched librarian.

*Tasche' Jackson*
*Virginia State University Woo Woo 2009-2010*

---

The most important piece of useful real woman advice I got from Dr. Johnson was, "If you give yourself constant credit, nobody else will." This quote has stuck with me because it was advice about humbleness. Doc always used Halle Berry as an example, so her analogy was "If Halle Berry told everyone that she was pretty all the time, no one else would say it to her." Humbleness is where blessings are created and is one of the reasons why we have had so many people supporting our organization through the years.

*Cozette Ford*
*Virginia State University Woo Woo 2001-2004*

PJ was a tremendous influence in my life. More than she ever knew. She saw things in us that we did not see in ourselves. She never wanted us to put up with mediocrity. Be the very best was what she always stressed. Work hard, work long, work smart and do it right. I still do all of this today. I try to use her influence today as I work with the young people as director of the dance ministry in my church. I want the reputation of my dance ministry to be as strong as the Woo Woos. Like PJ, I want them to be the best. It is paying off; my dance ministry is great, thanks to what I learned from PJ. I am instilling the same values she instilled in me.

*Sheila Smith Parker*
*Virginia State University Woo Woo 1975-1978*

---

The important piece of real woman advice I got from my Coach Doc, was to command everyone's attention by being bold, intelligent, beautiful, yet humble in spirit. Doc taught me not to follow the trends, but to make my mark in this world by setting them. Doc taught me to have ambition, and to be dedicated in whatever I do by giving 150% and not one percentage less. She taught me to be friendly and nice to everyone I meet because I may be entertaining an angel. I had the privilege of being one of her co-hosts on *Real Women ... Real Talk Radio*. I am who I am today because of Doc.

*Kristen Robinson*
*Virginia State University Woo Woo 1999-2002*

---

I learned through VSU and my cheerleader coach that family and a good education are the most important things in one's life. I clearly remember that Dr. Johnson (PJ was what we called her then) was very strict. She never allowed us to be anything less than the best we could be. From our hair to our shoes, we had to have it together or we were not allowed to cheer. She attended every single game and sat where she could see us as we performed. PJ would critique every move and if she saw a mistake, she demanded it be corrected the next game. Her kind of coaching made me a more confident and stronger person. I attribute my success as a mother, wife and a productive member of society mostly to Virginia State University and especially Dr. Johnson. If not for PJ's tough love I don't think I would have made it.

*Gwendolyn Gibbs Loftus*
*Virginia State University Woo Woo 1980-1981*

---

The most important piece of real woman advice I gained from my coach Doc, was to always put God first and foremost in everything. Doc constantly told all of us, to act like ladies. We knew we had better not be on the yard or anywhere else acting any other way. She also made sure we had our academics on point. Her words, her encouragement and the relationship we had with her are things that I know I will always cherish.

*Shekira Reynolds Hite*
*Virginia State University Woo Woo 1997-1999*

---

The most important advice I got from Dr. Johnson was about relationships. She said, "He's just not that into you." I was venting to her about my boyfriend's actions at the time and she simply told me the truth and she said he was treating me that way because he didn't want to be with me. That hurtful truth saved me from continuing an unhealthy relationship, even when all my friends were making excuses for his behavior. It was Dr. Johnson's truth that led me to become a real woman at an early age. I raised my son as a single parent and remain grateful for that truth.

*Dr. Shawnrell Blackwell*
*Virginia State University Woo Woo 1997-2000*

---

When I was cheering we were extremely popular. We were recognized as Woo Woos even when we were out of uniform and not cheering. PJ (that's what we called her then) told me to always be a lady in uniform and more importantly when I'm not in uniform. She told me that it was what I did out of the uniform that people would remember most.

*Brenda Wilkins-Norman*
*Virginia State University Woo Woo 1980-1983*

---

The most important piece of real woman advice I got from my coach (Doc) was to always remain true to myself and to be authentic. She insisted that I live in my truth as a cheerleader and as a result, I continue to live that way today. I was also fortunate to have been able to form a beautiful bond with Doc as one of her co-hosts on *Real Women…Real Talk Radio*. I consider it a blessing to get her real woman advice on a daily basis. Her real woman advice is advancing and molding me in so many ways.

*Antoinette "Toni" Jackson*
*Virginia State University Woo Woo 2004-2007*

My high school cheerleading squad was coached by the school's football coach. Ninety percent of the training I got was the same as the football team. By the time I got to Virginia State University and tried out, I was surprised at how physically weak most the girls trying out with me were. Since PJ was a hardnosed stickler for executing good skills and fitness, I knew right away that I'd like her for a coach. She drilled us on the importance of resolving our differences and so we established the "lemon squeeze" which was a closed session to put our "issues" on the table. What I learned from that is now called, "agreeing to disagree". This concept is currently being taught in leadership classes. Imagine how smart I felt in class when it was first introduced. Little did my leadership classmates know that I had learned and executed the concept years before as a Woo Woo at VSU.

PJ was an inspiration to all of us, especially those of us who were battling our own identity and what contributions we wanted to make to society. She just seemed to know exactly what she wanted and how to execute a plan to get it. She had and still has a strong personality; that, as I look back, most people would not challenge. Just strong willed I'd say. But, under that tough, my way or the highway, wouldn't bend exterior, she had a heart of platinum. She had a way of making everyone feel that they were special. That's what makes my experience with PJ so unique. She just wanted all of us to be who we were and to love ourselves.

*Stacy Davis Boseman*
*Virginia State University Woo Woo 1975-1979*

To start, I must say that Paulette Walker Johnson has molded me into the woman I am today. She tailors her advice to fit any woman; past, present and future. What stuck with me was her advice to "put your big girl draws on". Many people say this phrase, but coming from her, made me realize I had to wipe my tears, hold my head up and keep it moving. And if I get off track, I can hear her voice in my head saying, "Is ya been?" All in all, this phenomenal woman has been sent from God to break down and explain a "real" message. I am grateful that I was able to have grown from it.

*Cassandra Artis-Williams*
*Virginia State University Woo Woo 2010-2012*

---

The most important piece of real woman advice I got from my coach Doc, is to recognize my beauty on the inside and out. When I became a Woo Woo, I was young, and very insecure. Doc not only gave me words of advice, but led by the example she set of how to be a confident, self-assured woman.

*Robin Gray Pelt*
*Virginia State University Woo Woo 1988-1991*

## My Coach...My Advisor

**D** – designs strong black women
**R** – represents a woman, I hope to someday become
**P** – preaches self respect
**A** – always gives me good advice on life
**U** – ultimately wants nothing but the best for me
**L** – levels with me even when no one else will
**E** – emphasizes to always love yourself
**T** – teaches me that I am beautiful
**T** – talks about self presentation in any situation
**E** – expresses to always set high standards for yourself
**W** – willingly gives unselfishly
**J** – just loves us "Woo Woos"
**O** – openly shares of herself when needed
**H** – honestly will tell me what I need and should have
**N** – never settle for less than perfection
**S** – shows by example
**O** – opposes lies, stresses that one should
  "just tell the truth"
**N** – notices character, before she even
  really knows you

*Tawanna Tynes-McClain*
*Virginia State University Woo Woo 1994-1997*

127

# About the Author

Dr. Paulette Walker Johnson is an associate professor at Virginia State University where she spent 35 years coaching the nationally recognized Virginia State University "Woo-Woos" Cheering Squad. Setting the standard for HBCU cheering programs, the Woo Woos and Dr. Johnson were featured on the BET television network, Urban Sports Network and ESPN. In the 1990s the squad performed at a boxing match staged by the legendary promoter Don King. In 1999, the mayor of Petersburg, Virginia(The Honorable Rosalyn Dance) established, "Dr. Paulette Walker Johnson Day"in recognition of her service to Virginia State University and the Public School Board.

Dr. Johnson is noted as the first female athletic director in VSU history. She was the first president and founder of the CIAA Cheerleader Coaches Association; and in 2011 became the first cheerleader coach ever inducted into the CIAA Hall of Fame.

Dr. Paulette Walker Johnson is the creator and host of the radio talk show, *Real Women ... Real Talk* on Virginia State University's The Source 91.3 FM WVST and on Sirius XM Channel 142, HBCU. She is a motivational speaker who lectures and facilitates workshops throughout the East Coast. Her areas of expertise include fitness, wellness and of course, real women issues. She is a graduate of Morgan State University, Springfield College and Virginia Tech.

# *Contact Information*

If you would like to schedule a speaking engagement
with the author, contact publicist, E.J. Simmons at:
lyfelonglearner@gmail.com.

For additional information about
Real Women ... Real Talk,
visit the website at:
www.realwomenrealtalk.net

CPSIA information can be obtained
at www.ICGtesting.com
Printed in the USA
LVHW052359240520
656497LV00002B/290